The Second Family

Also by Dr. Ron Taffel

Getting Through to Difficult Kids and Parents:
Uncommon Sense for Child Professionals

Also by Dr. Ron Taffel with Melinda Blau

Nurturing Good Children Now: 10 Basic Skills
to Protect and Strengthen Your Child's Core

Parenting by Heart: How to Be in Charge,
Stay Connected, and Instill Your Values
When It Feels Like You've Got Only 15 Minutes a Day

By Dr. Ron Taffel with Roberta Israeloff

Why Parents Disagree and What You
Can Do About It: How to Raise Great Kids
While You Strengthen Your Marriage

By Melinda Blau

Families Apart: Ten Keys to Successful Coparenting

Loving and Listening: A Parent's Book of Daily
Inspirations for Rebuilding the Family After Divorce

Also Coauthored by Melinda Blau

Secrets of the Baby Whisperer:
How to Calm, Connect, and Communicate with Your Baby
(with Tracy Hogg)

Watch Me Fly: What I Learned on My Way
to Becoming the Woman I Was Meant to Be
(with Myrlie Evers Williams)

Our Turn: Women Who Triumph in the Face of Divorce
(with Dr. Christopher Hayes and Deborah Anderson)

The Second Family

How Adolescent Power
Is Challenging
the American Family

Dr. Ron Taffel

with Melinda Blau

Please be advised:
Contains explicit language and sexual material

ST. MARTIN'S PRESS ⚏ NEW YORK

www.stmartins.com

Permissions acknowledgements:

Excerpt from "The Sopranos." Courtesy of Home Box Office.

Lyrics from "Break It On Down" by 2 Live Crew. Written by Mark Ross, Luther Campbell, David Hobbs, and Chris Wong Won. Courtesy of Lil' Joe Records, Inc.

Library of Congress Cataloging-in-Publication Data

Taffel, Ron.
    The second family : how adolescent power is challenging the American family / Ron Taffel with Melinda Blau.—1st ed.
        p. cm.
    "Why kids are creating their own families and how adults can prevent them from slipping away."
    ISBN 0-312-26137-3
    1. Teenagers—Social networks.   2. Parent and teenager.   3. Popular culture. I. Blau, Melinda.   II. Title.
    HQ796 .T316   2001   00-045993
    306.874—dc21   CIP

First Edition: March 2001

10   9   8   7   6   5   4   3   2   1

To Leah and Sam,
Jennifer and Jeremy

Contents

A Note to the Reader   ix

Prologue
"Welcome to the Fun House"   3
Seeing Ourselves Through Adolescents' Eyes

1. "What the Hell Is Going On?"   6
Why We Don't Know Our Kids

2. "You Adults Don't Have a Clue"   32
Understanding the Second Family

3. "I'm Not Who You Think I Am"   53
The Two Faces of Teens

4. "Why Don't You Invite Your Friends Over?"   73
Dealing with the Second Family

5. "Don't Let Me Slip Away"   103
Lying and the Empathic Envelope

6. "Listen to Me!"   118
Increasing Empathy and Self-Reflection

7. "How Dare You!"   134
*Dealing with Privacy, Confidentiality,
and Other Matters of Trust*

8. "Don't You Grownups Ever Talk to Each Other?"   161
Creating Adult Partnerships to Protect Kids

Appendix
Parent-School Partnership Initiatives   189
Specific Guidelines for Successful Programs

Acknowledgments   203

About the Authors   205

A Note to the Reader

About the Book

It is almost impossible to stop writing *The Second Family*. Every day I hear about new and often totally outrageous adolescent behavior and, at the same time, I hear stories about our kids that are equally inspiring. Working with twenty-first-century teenagers is like riding one of those 360-degree monster roller coasters. It defies gravity, moves at unthinkable, heart-stopping speed, and there's no getting off. Once you're strapped in, as my wife, Stacey, and I are, having a teen and preteen ourselves, there's no turning back.

Every day, parents and educators reel from this same experience, feeling themselves up against a new adolescence so powerful few are prepared to effectively deal with it. In the face of this challenge I've set three basic goals for *The Second Family*: first, to describe in accessible terms a phenomenon that affects all teens but until now has had no name; second, to offer a no-holds-barred look inside the second family — its excesses as well as its surprising strengths; and third, to suggest a new paradigm — the empathic envelope — along with concrete solutions that can be used by all adults who deal with teens today.

About the People

The illustrations I give throughout *The Second Family* are based on real people. However, to protect their privacy I have disguised every example. Many are composites of several situations. Still others are taken from experiences I've heard about dozens, if not hundreds, of times. My aim is to capture the essence of these stories without providing identifying information.

About the Language

To describe modern teen and preteen life, I had to be true to the casual, raunchy way adolescents speak and to their often precocious sexual behavior. As a writer of four childrearing books, countless articles for *McCall's* and *Parents* magazines, and in the thousand workshops I have led, I do not curse. Growing up in my mother's and father's house, cursing was unthinkable and it is something Stacey and I feel strongly about with our own kids.

I apologize, then, if I offend any reader. It wasn't easy putting some of these words on paper and, as the parent of two children, even harder describing the explicit sexuality of our young people. In fact, if I erred in any direction, it was to *tone down* the language and leave out some of the more extreme, and therefore less common, behaviors I know about.

In a way, though, adult discomfort doesn't really matter. Whether we like it or not, this half-crazed world is what it is. To be realistic about kids today, we can't wish ourselves back to a more civil time.

About the Research

The Second Family is based on a wide spectrum of interviews with kids of all ages, across socioeconomic groups, in both normal and dysfunctional families; it includes children and adults I have spoken with in schools, treated in counseling, supervised in the not-for-profit agency I direct, or met at the workshops I've conducted around the country. Literally thousands of voices are represented here.

Although adults may not be completely comfortable with what is written in these pages, the observations offered are drawn from an extensive and varied population. The many voices recorded ought to be heard, for they are sending a clear message. To reckon with adolescent power, a strong empathic envelope needs to be created: we must balance empathy and expectations, so that kids feel held by the first family at home.

About Public Policy

While the empathic envelope can help all parents and adults who deal with teens, it also suggests a balance that has implications for community institutions—schools and houses of worship—as well as the world of pop culture.

We live, thankfully, under the protection of the First Amendment. But families struggle daily because of the impact of pop culture images and its ethos. Hopefully, discussion about these struggles may contribute to greater awareness and constructive action that will enable parents to better guide our children.

This is no simple task, for grownups or for teens. But, despite its dangers and stark realities, *The Second Family* is about hope—kids are better and adults potentially far more effective than most of us can possibly imagine.

The Empathic Envelope:
balancing empathy and expectations, so that
kids feel held by the first family at home.

The Second Family

PROLOGUE

"Welcome to the Fun House"
Seeing Ourselves Through Adolescents' Eyes

In their shocking and sometimes frightening behavior, in the rules of their private world, and in the longing of their hearts, teenagers are telling us everything we need to know, not just about themselves, but about ourselves.

You may look at teenagers today with a mixture of amazement and disgust. If so, you're in for a shock: What you see is actually a reflection of what's going on in the adult world—the good *and* the bad. Then again, you might choose not to see it, as is the case with many adults, or you might miss the similarities. The effect is the equivalent of looking at oneself in a fun-house mirror. You see a distorted and exaggerated view of the person you are. But look again carefully, and you'll find that teens today are not so much rebelling against adult life, but taking it to an extreme. In effect, while modern adolescent life is evidence of how far we've evolved in some arenas, it also mirrors some of the most alienating, materialistic, and dangerous cultural trends in society—taken a giant step further with emblematic teenage flair.

As we are victims of a consumer culture and drive ourselves to attain possessions—the best cars, houses, TVs, clothes, and other worldly goods, not to mention the hottest stocks—our children are stricken by "the gimmees," an unrelenting need for the artifacts of the pop culture and the erroneous assumption that things buy happiness.

As we overschedule our own days and become more dismissive of, and distant from, one another and our children than our hearts would like, kids are disengaging from us at earlier and earlier ages.

As we choose career over family and spend increasing amounts of time away from home, children are spending more and more time away from home as well, choosing peers over parents and distancing themselves to the point of inhabiting an alternate reality.

As we make friends at work instead of communing with our neighbors, a phenomenon sociologist Arlie Hochschild documented in *The Time Bind*, our kids are making friends at school and in cyberspace—and, as a result, spending time with children whom we often don't get to meet.

As we have become increasingly individualistic and isolated, lacking ties to a larger community and caring mostly about whatever makes our own lives comfortable and full, children have become more egocentric, too. At worst, they care little about others' feelings and believe that the world revolves around their needs.

As we feel alienated and frustrated and find ourselves unable to deal with the illness, loneliness, financial problems, and forgetfulness of our own parents, our children—off in their own separate universe—lose patience with us. They are also unable and, often, unwilling, to communicate with their elders.

As our relationships falter and marriages are in crisis because of an inability to manage conflict, express feelings, and respect each other's vulnerabilities, children are exhibiting a disturbing tendency toward cruelty, confrontation, and violence with their peers.

As we seek relief from stress by drinking or by taking prescribed and natural remedies, children are altering their chemistry, too, experimenting and—at shockingly early ages—getting into trouble with drugs and alcohol.

As more adults seek physical perfection through exercise routines, diets, and plastic surgery, kids are becoming similarly obsessed with redefining their own bodies. In teenagers, this is expressed through tattooing and multiple piercing, various types of eating disorders, and, at the most extreme, self-mutilation.

As we take in stride the widespread and explicit images of sexuality used to sell products, our children are becoming sexually active and highly experimental at earlier and earlier ages. By the time they graduate high school, a majority of adolescents have had sex.

It is also true that teenagers have incorporated in their own lives and behavior some of the more *positive* reflections of the adult culture — the caring and sharing movement — which has led to a proliferation of support networks; the increased openness and a recognition of the importance of relationships; a greater awareness of compulsive behavior and addiction; better understanding across gender lines; an acknowledgment of the need to achieve balance in one's life; a trend toward diversity and acceptance — a widespread live-and-let-live mentality.

Thus, in their most shocking and often frightening behavior, in the rules of their private world, as well as in the longing of their hearts, teenagers are telling us everything we need to know, not just about them, but about ourselves. By peering thoughtfully and bravely into their universe, adults can find answers that will heal our families, restore our schools, and strengthen our communities.

Over time, and with many false starts and disappointments, we may make enough of a difference to challenge this maddening legacy.

1

"What the Hell Is Going On?"

Why We Don't Know Our Kids

Most parents don't understand their teenagers. A powerful force—the second family—is wrenching them from their families at home and changing the very nature of adolescence. Teens are angrier, more sexual, and their behavior more outrageous. They value comfort above all and worship celebrity. A new paradigm of parenting is called for, requiring adults to honor and understand this "second family" and to build a bridge so that kids can find their way home.

Caution: Alarming Content Ahead

We don't understand our children. This is a bitter pill for parents and educators to swallow—adults who look for answers in today's headlines as much as in books about child psychology. They read about violence in schools and about kids who kill, and they become preoccupied. "Will my child be next? Can a child in my classroom be the next to explode? Is this child or that capable of murder?" But they're asking the wrong questions and looking in the wrong places for answers. This book isn't going to ponder the question, "Why do kids kill?" It isn't going to explain why violence occupies front and center stage in America (despite the ironic fact that, statistically, the incidence of violence is actually *down*). In contrast, this book is about the vast majority of kids in the middle, the kids in your home, your classroom, or on your playing field, who will probably never even touch a gun, much less put a bullet through anyone's heart.

Make no mistake: The kids in the middle are getting into trouble, too—often, serious trouble, with sex, drugs, vandalism, extreme risk-taking—but their outrageous acts rarely make the headlines. Sometimes, their own parents won't even find out. And those teens are the ones I'm most concerned about.

Adults are aware that children are somehow slipping away. They search for solutions in books about boys, in books about girls, in books about morality. They point fingers at each other, blaming themselves for not being strict enough. Or, they level charges at schools for not being more strict or at the media for serving up images to their kids that cause them to spin out of control. In truth, though, the real problem is quite simple:

Although most parents love their children, they aren't able to pay the right kind of attention to them. As I will explain later, we have seen the demise of so-called undivided time. No matter how hard they try, many parents don't really hear their children. They don't really see them. They don't know enough about the world their children inhabit, their interests, their motives. They know even less about adolescence, because too many of their children, as young as twelve or thirteen, have already drifted away from them.

If you've read this far, you might be inclined to put this book back on the shelf. As a parent, I can understand why. I don't want to believe that I don't know my own children, who are now fourteen and a half and almost ten, one a budding adolescent, the other soon to be. The notion that we have lost touch with our kids is, as a parent, painful to feel. And, as a professional, it's painful to write. To be sure, most magazine and book editors would prefer my putting a more positive "spin" on this story, lest I scare readers away. But I simply can't gloss over what's happening with teenagers today.

In my previous books, in fact, my tone has always been reassuring. I've acted as a guide to childhood, offering parents pointers that will help them navigate the terrain. Ten years ago, when I wrote my first book, *Parenting by Heart,* my goal was to help parents connect with their children. In the intervening years, however, the road has taken an unexpected turn, and we have now reached a critical crossroad in history, which has literally made obsolete most of the tried-and-true notions about families. Today, there's no hope of connecting unless parents first get to know who their kids are.

Hence, we must begin at square one. It's time to look at and listen to what's *really* happening in kids' lives. Acquaint yourself with what I call "the new adolescence." Today's teenagers aren't the disaffected hoods of the 1958 classic, *Blackboard Jungle*, or the rebellious hippies of the '60s. These kids—boys *and* girls—have a completely different mind-set from their forebears, an elastic live-and-let-live sense of morality that governs how they behave. Peer pressure, as we once knew it, is dead; teens don't get into trouble because friends put them up to it. Celebrities are the new deities.

Adolescence has also gotten younger. As early as first or second grade, children are influenced by the *tyranny of cool*, a standard bearer of the pop culture that we formerly associated solely with teens. By the time kids do reach adolescence, their key motivation is not rebellion, but *comfort*. Adolescents today don't rebel out of revenge or anger toward their parents. They are merely drifting away, desperate to find a place— where they're known and where they feel comfortable.

Although I will offer strategies and solutions later in the book, my primary goal here is to encourage you to start thinking differently. Just as the business world is shifting from an "old economy" to a new paradigm, so are our social lives and our children's. Rather than applying "old-think" principles, then, you need to shift your perspective, see who kids really are, what they're dealing with, and what spurs them in their day-to-day existence. Ultimately, my hope is to help you to increase your capacity for empathy, but to do that, you have to see things as they are, not as you want them to be. And I warn you, what you're about to learn is not for the faint of heart.

Welcome to Planet Youth

Consider, for example, Jessica, the child of middle-class professionals living in suburbia. She has just been told by her mother to stop watching TV and to clean up the table for dinner.

"Not now," Jessica says, without bothering to look up.

"No, Jessica," counters her mother sharply. "I mean this minute."

"Later," Jessica responds, almost absentmindedly.

Mom stiffens and threatens: "Stop it now or there won't be TV tonight." Finally, she's got her daughter's attention.

Jessica looks her mother squarely in the face and says, "Fuck you, Mommy."

Jessica is eight years old. And she is far from unique.

■

Adults who encounter kids today—parents, teachers, counselors, therapists—are confused and angered by similar outbursts in their own homes and schools and offices. Exchanges like this, along with far more serious infractions, have become entwined in the fabric of everyday family life. The father of another eight-year-old tells me that when he asked his son for the fourth time to turn off the computer game and straighten his room, the boy shot back, "Leave me alone, Butthead!" I hear the "flailing tantrum" story over and over, too: a parent directs a child not to chew gum or to stop playing and get ready for bed. The child responds by hurling him- or herself at the parent, thrashing with small, angry fists.

It's not just the anger. It's the disdain for adults. It's the disconnection from their own families. It's the incomprehensible disregard for anyone who isn't in their world. It's the sliding moral scale, which allows kids to rationalize and disengage. Of course, I see the casualties in my office. But it's not just boys and girls in therapy. I've interviewed hundreds of children, heard about thousands more through parenting workshops and school consultations. And I'm not only referring to those who are guilty of garden-variety youthful infractions—kids who pick on the class geek or the ones who are constantly rude to their teachers. It's also the kids who set fire to or vandalize buildings without an ounce of guilt or remorse. It's the high school kids who are into day trading on the Internet, already consumed by a corporate warrior mentality. It's the fourteen-year-olds who are having sex with each other in the school bathroom and don't care who walks in on them. It's the thirteen-year-old girl on the way home from a class trip who gave a boy a blow job in the back of a school bus while her fellow eighth-graders watched. It's the boy who became a pimp in seventh grade and the girls who worked for him. It's the group of kids who've broken into an abandoned warehouse to hold "x-treme" wrestling events—which don't end until one of the participants is left unconscious.

The teenagers I meet have made me aware that parents—all adults— must change their thinking and how they deal with today's kids. Sure, teenagers have always set themselves apart, broken the rules, irritated grownups. But these kids are a mystery to most parents—and our demands are equally mysterious to them.

Patricia, for example, a mother in Chicago, recently told me about an exasperating moment with her thirteen-year-old daughter. Julie hadn't been involved in any major difficulties except for early signs of an eating disorder that seemed a year later to be under control. But then Patricia found out that Julie was hanging out after school with a group of kids whose parents were never home. "I told her that I wouldn't permit it, and that she simply wasn't allowed to be unsupervised in mixed company," Patricia recounted. "And she just stared at me in disbelief, as if she didn't understand why I would even lay down such a rule—almost like it wasn't any of my business." Patricia went on to explain that Julie didn't seem angry, nor did she try to argue or start bargaining. She just looked at her mother and said, "That seems so stupid. I can do anything I want, go any place I want. What's the difference if there are no adults around?"

Julie's lack of comprehension about her mother's "right" to lay down a rule resonates a universal trend. It is clear to me that teenagers today are flying farther from the family than any generation before them, redefining adolescence in the bargain. Witness this conversation:

Boy: Do you want to hook up?
Girl: No, I'm not interested.
Boy: Yeah, well you can go lick my balls instead.
Girl: Listen, where your balls should be, someone ought to put up a "vacancy" sign.

Boy: You sound like you're reading from some soft-core porno script, you skank-bitch.

Girl: Listen, dickhead, the answer is still "No!"

That this discussion occurred between heartland twelve-year-olds — honor students to boot — speaks volumes about the new adolescence. It certainly is not surprising that their parents often can't reach these teenagers; that their teachers have trouble teaching them; or that their coaches and counselors don't really understand them. They rarely seem part of our world. Instead, our adolescents are the willing inhabitants of Planet Youth — which, to outsiders (read: adults), seems no more than a materialistic, kid-centered universe where instant gratification reigns. It isn't quite that simple. In fact, teenagers feel supported by their private universe. It is a place where they're given a kind of understanding and succor that they don't always find at home.

Jared, for one, fits the profile of the new adolescent. A fourteen-year-old, he wears his hair long and unkempt, his army-issue T-shirt frayed at the edges, and his too-large jeans slung so low that his underwear peeks out. Jared has been courting expulsion from eighth grade because of his obvious, but heatedly denied, pot-smoking. To his parents' horror, his fashion statement also includes multiple piercings. A skull and crossbones dangle from his left earlobe, a dagger penetrates his eyebrow, and an Egyptian ankh projects from his lower lip — "for good luck," he explains. Despite appearances, Jared is no street kid. The only child of affluent, caring parents, he attends a school that could be anywhere in Suburbia, U.S.A. But everything he does — painting his room black, his low-rent look, the piercings — seems to shout to his parents, "Stay away! I'm not part of your world and I don't want you in mine." It's no wonder that Jared's ability to use, sell, and distribute all manner of illegal substances remained a mystery to the adults in his life.

Every day, in my office, I see boys like Jared, or their female counterparts — a girl like thirteen-year-old Sara, who dresses in scanty knit tops and microminis and teeters in chunky heels. Unbeknownst to her parents, she has a "GRRRL" tattoo on her right hip — the result of a secret outing with her girlfriends last summer at camp. And, she has recently pierced her nipple, a fact she divulges with great joy and self-satisfaction. It is one of many steps she's taken in her young life that her parents are absolutely clueless about—and that, more than the tattoo or the piercing, is the real source of my alarm. Sara is flying solo in a cosmos that includes few adults. Her frail frame and baby-soft skin notwithstanding, she has the mien of a young adult, someone who's seen it all. That she's doing poorly in school concerns her far less than her popularity. Like teenagers of old, she talks on the phone endlessly. What is different, though, is that while Mom and Dad are successfully baricaded out of her private domain, Sara can talk to seven people simultaneously—juggling two friends on call waiting, five others in private chat rooms on-line. Meanwhile the TV and her CD player drone on as background noise—a cacophony of deep base rhythms and casually obscene lyrics.

Let loose in their own world, which is both driven and supported by technological forces unlike anything we've ever experienced, young people have no reason to stage an uprising or to rebel against family values. They are, in many ways, already gone, immersed in what I call the second family—the aggregate force of the pop culture and the peer group.

Having been raised on movies and sitcoms that reinforce the idea that parents are, for the most part, dorky and, therefore, must be tolerated, they are often too impatient with their elders if not downright rude. "What an asshole!" mutters a ten-year-old under her breath, when her mother instructs her to finish her homework before turning on the TV. How striking and how different from the days of *Father Knows Best*—a time when adults were obeyed (at least superficially) simply because they were adults. Today younger-than-ever kids seem to ask their parents and other adults in their life to let them be. They want the freedom to hang out with their friends and to heed the call of the pop culture.

The Ostrich Factor

What is amazing—and different now—is this: *Parents of teens and even many preteens rarely know much about their kids' involvements and less about their misdeeds.* This is both because parents bury their heads in the sand and because there's an unwritten code on Planet Youth, a conspiracy of silence, whereby kids manage to keep from most adults just about everything they or their friends do. The only exception is a life-and-death situation, when a peer is literally teetering on the brink of disaster; then kids *may* turn to a grownup.

"Isn't Dawn worried about her mother's reaction?" I naively wondered out loud when eleven-year-old Amy told me that her friend had had her belly button pierced and a ring inserted.

"Of course not. Her mother will never know," Amy told me confidently.

Six months later and still counting, Dawn's mother *is* none the wiser. This, sadly, is often the case — unless something absolutely disastrous occurs, which is precisely what happened at a recent Midwestern suburban junior high school graduation. For the past several years, without any adults being aware of the tradition, graduates had taken to celebrating their passage into high school by jumping off a fifty-foot bridge into a river below. This particular year, though, among the graduates was a girl who was secretly anorexic, and when she jumped, she broke her back.

Perhaps you're thinking, *My child would never do such things.* Many parents are dismissive when I share such stories. "My child would never lie to me," they insist, or "My child tells me everything." Or perhaps you're like some of my own friends, who claim that I "worry too much," when I question whether there will be adult supervision at a party that my thirteen-year-old daughter is pleading to attend.

"What could go on?" they challenge.

What indeed! I have firsthand knowledge that proves how wrong my friends are. Maybe it's an occupational hazard — I'm paid not to be an ostrich — but one adolescent after another comes to me, relating stories that make my hair curl. I know that children tell prodigious, bold-faced lies to their parents. I know that most teens today are capable of saying and doing things their parents would never in their wildest dreams imagine. When, for instance, kids talk about "hooking up" — a term that sounds innocent enough to us parents — they don't mean hanging around or going steady. They may just as well mean sex. And at so-called make-out parties, where once the daring acts included copping a feel and French kissing, now kids as young as eleven or twelve are giving "hand jobs"; in junior high, they're having oral sex and a surprising number even engage in group sex. In one such group sex "club," early adolescents engage in anal as well as oral sex—all in the name of maintaining the status of "virgin."

Admittedly, I hear stories from kids that I don't want to believe about other people's children, much less about my own! For instance, I flash on Steven, the fifteen-year-old boy who schemed so elaborately with his friends, so carefully laying one bit of subterfuge on top of another, that he was able to travel all the way across the country to visit a girlfriend. Only because he missed his flight home did his parents ultimately find out that Steven wasn't where he said he'd be. I recall fourteen-year-old Liz who had her tongue pierced—of course, without her parents' knowledge—and explained in a nonchalant tone, "So that I can give better head." And I think of the group of nameless thirteen- and fourteen-year-olds in the Southeast whose parents sponsored a religious retreat in the wilderness and never found out that their kids had sneaked off en masse to smoke pot and drop acid. It didn't occur to these kids that their behavior was counterproductive to the goal of the retreat, which was to increase their spiritual connection. It just happened—no big deal.

Rethinking Adolescent Anger

Teenagers' exploits don't shock me quite as much as they did a few years ago, when I first began listening to such stories. Then I was at my professional wit's end. I kept trying the old methods of "getting through"—asking the right questions and suggesting possible causes for kids' acting-out behavior, whatever form it took. My goal, typical of most therapists, was to somehow find a common ground and make a connection with the teen. But more often than not, my probing was met with either uninterested stares or disbelief. I might just as well have been talking in tongues.

I was not alone in my confusion about kids' behavior. A widow living in Florida was aghast when, during a routine call to her granddaughter, the child interrupted her, saying, "I'm not finished talking yet, Grandma—just cool it!" In her day, even in her daughter's day, no child would have dared to talk to a grandparent in such a disrespectful tone. In interviews with other therapists as well as important adults in kids' lives—teachers, coaches, principals, community leaders, camp owners—I've heard the same disturbing patterns of anger toward adults, manifested not by hulking high school wrestlers or grunge kids, but sometimes by the tiniest, most innocent-looking tykes. One fellow clinician told me that a preteen girl he had been seeing expressed her jealousy of an unborn sibling not by the usual array of anticipatory anxieties, but by smashing a baseball bat into her mother's pregnancy-swollen belly.

Other therapists point out that it is becoming commonplace for middle schoolers or even younger kids to look them dead in the eye, say, "Who do you think you are?" and then march out of the session. A longtime camp director says that the biggest concerns of his fellow members of a national camping association were no longer issues of homesickness, but of wild acting out—flagrant disrespect toward counselors and public sexual behaviors by even preteens. At nationwide symposia, this new adolescence occupies center stage in workshop presentations. The clergy are not even immune. One group of young teens, boys and girls at a religious camp, "mooned" the stunned minister as he rode by. An eminent children's theater director said that in twenty-five years of producing plays, he has seen increasing disrespect for him and his colleagues by his young charges. "I can't describe the enormity of change in the way children behave. I can no longer count on having their respect and attention merely because I am the adult and a teacher. Now half the struggle is just to get them to begin to listen to my directions."

Nothing in my training prepared me to deal with children raised in today's world—children who, in large part, have defected from their own families and sought refuge in the pop culture and in their peers. As a parent I was alarmed, knowing that a major shift was happening in our culture, which would eventually affect my family as well. Way before school violence exploded across America, I began a search for answers. Why, I asked myself, are kids so angry and distant? What is going on that is so wrong between adults and children, often making it seem as if we are walking in a minefield? Despite the many solutions that I and other parenting authors have come up with over the last decade, are we missing something?

Discovering the Second Family

I initiated a three-pronged search. First, I combed the professional literature of the last thirty years for clues, hoping to ascertain what, if anything, has been consistently regarded by child researchers as critical for raising emotionally healthy children. Next, I reviewed my own twenty-five years' worth of work with families, doing therapy, teaching, supervising other therapists, presenting at more than a thousand workshops, and, not so incidentally, writing for parents themselves in my books and in columns for *Parents* and *McCall's* magazines. Finally, and perhaps most important, I talked to the kids themselves. Initially, I interviewed 150 preschool through middle school children.* As the cumulative effect of listening to what was really happening in kids' lives began to weigh on me, I then broadened my study to include more than a hundred adolescents. Although there was a massive convergence among all the sources, in my search for answers, the children themselves were the ones who gave me the greatest insight about their needs and how parents — in fact, most adults — were failing them.

Coincidentally, around this time, I had already started offering teenagers the chance to bring their friends to therapy with them and most willingly agreed. After all, as a family therapist, I had been trained to view individuals as part of a "system." Seeing parents and siblings was standard practice, but, now, realizing how important peers were, I knew I had to see friends as well. I realized that a kid's friends comprised a kind of extended family.

Listening both to kids who came to my office with specific problems and to the schoolchildren I interviewed, I began to see that *before* adolescence, starting in late elementary school, youngsters tend to move

---

*The results of interviews with younger kids are reported in *Nurturing Good Children Now* (St. Martin's Press, 1999).

away from their own siblings and parents. They surround themselves instead with friends, forming a second, separate but equally important, system. As kids become more and more attached to their friends and to the common interests they share, by early adolescence, it is a natural, easy step to divorce themselves not only from their first families but, often, from other significant adults as well.

That even young kids share a world outside the one at home should not be surprising. Modern kids' time, their passions, and their conversations are shaped en masse by media-inspired messages. According to a 1999 Kaiser Family Foundation report, *Kids and the Media*, "Children's bedrooms are rapidly becoming 'media central,' offering most kids the chance to consume many kinds of media in the privacy of their own rooms." A majority of all children, the report notes, have radios, tape players, TVs or CD players in their bedrooms; a third have video-game players and VCRs as well. These figures rise when you look at children eight and older; two-thirds (65 percent) have a TV and 21 percent a computer in their bedroom. And parents are almost never involved. In the diaries of kids seven and older who kept track of their media use, when they are engaged with media, *95 percent of the time they're not with their parents.* It's no wonder that middle school children and teenagers repeatedly tell me that their parents have no idea what they're up to. For as long and as late as they like, they listen to music, watch programs, or visit Internet sites that their parents know little or nothing about. This leaves them in their own universe, where loyalty is less to their own families than to the kid culture and the closed society of their peers.

Sitting with their friends, teenagers are surprisingly willing to talk about their world; I guess there is safety in numbers. Meeting with groups of kids in this way helped me begin to grasp the idea that "a second family," as I labeled this collective force of peers and pop culture, was capturing children's attention and allegiance at earlier and earlier ages. Unfortunately, parents weren't providing much resistance. After all, it's hard to resist what you don't recognize — a phenomenon that doesn't have a name.

The Demise of Undivided Attention

It's an old story by now that massive changes in society—divorce, increased mobility, and economic pressure forcing both parents to work—have chipped away at the foundations of the family. But from the kid's eye view, the damage in real-life terms is even worse than we'd like to believe. Parents struggling to find enough hours in the day to meet the competing demands of work and parenthood often let everyday routines slip by the wayside. It's no wonder that almost every one of the children and teens I interviewed for my second-family study told me that they missed the mundane rituals that make up family life—dinner together, pancakes on Sunday, regular trips to the playground. "I want my mommy to lie down with me every night," said one child. "Last week my mom and dad took me bowling and it was great!" said another, wishing that such special times could happen more often.

Listening to these children, it is relatively easy to understand why the *second family* has become so much more powerful than the first—a child's family of origin. Many of my young interviewees told me that their parents simply weren't around or they were preoccupied. "We don't spend time together in my family," a fifth-grader told me, succinctly echoing a condition that almost every child I've ever interviewed has described. It became obvious that it's not just that parents are out of the house more often—it's that even when everyone's home, "shared" family time is not what it used to be.

This is devastating for parents to hear, especially working parents who care deeply about their children and try to put them at the center of their universe. Oddly enough, studies indicate that we aren't actually spending less time with kids than we did in the '60s. The problem is that for all our child-focused intentions, we're spending "divided time." In a typical evening, Mom and Dad watch television in the living room, while Junior is watching his own program in his room—often, with his music blaring as well. Sis is playing with her Little Mermaid toy while she watches *Sabrina, The Teenage Witch* on *her* television set. You may think I'm exaggerating. Yet, the Kaiser Foundation study found that 32 percent of two- to seven-year-olds have their own TV sets. Parents who kept diaries about these younger kids admitted that 81 percent of the time when their kids are watching TV, the adults are doing something else.

Even worse, everyone nowadays — including parents — seems to do ten things at once. You've seen kids doing homework with headphones on, or talking on the phone while they fold socks? But before we criticize our kids, we ought to look in the mirror. In most American homes it's not unusual to see Mom diapering the baby while cradling a receiver between her chin and neck. In another room, Dad "multitasks," to use a catchphrase of the last decade (originally intended to describe computer functioning): he simultaneously checks his E-mail messages and his stock portfolio on the computer while yelling out to the children, "Start cutting the vegetables for tonight's dinner!" It's not surprising that a 1997 *Family Circle* report found that fathers spend only eight minutes a day talking to their children and working mothers, eleven.

There is nothing inherently evil about any of this — it's normal family life in America — but it's no way to get to know your own children, or each other. Kids understand this. In my conversations with them, children from kindergarten to age twelve overwhelmingly indicate that what they want most is more time, as in *undivided* attention. I repeatedly hear comments such as, "I want my mom to stop being so busy and just play with me" and "I love when my dad sits next to me and we watch movies together."

Interestingly, although almost all kids recognize this loss, their reaction to it changes as they get older. At first, they are sad, even angry, because they're not getting undivided time. They yearn for it. But by the end of elementary school, as the second family slowly begins to take a firmer hold on a child's interests and values, I hear a defiant acceptance. "That's just the way it is . . ." many kids say, "my parents are busy . . . it's okay . . ."

In part, harried parents aren't making or taking the time. In part, they're worried about not doing enough to enrich their kids' lives and to give them the edge they'll need in a changing world. Unconsciously competing with the fast-action, high-tech offerings of the pop culture, modern mothers and fathers are desperate not to "bore" children with so-called old-fashioned activities, like arts and crafts, or "impose" on them an unexciting trip to Grandma's house. So, instead of playing a game of catch with his daughter on Saturday afternoon, Dad chauffeurs her to a soccer club. The sad irony is that although parents believe they're enriching their kids' lives, they're actually depriving them of what the kids want most in elementary school: one-on-one time with Mom or Dad.

Thus, the *quality* of family life has changed dramatically. Even when parents are home with their kids, they're less connected to them and, as a result, the first family—with parents at the center—exerts less of a gravitational pull on children. It's not that parents aren't trying to exert influence on their children, or to rein them in. It's that they have few ideas about how. There's little weight on parents' side, little pull. Many mothers and fathers throw up their hands in despair. Almost nothing they do seems to have the same effect as the second family.

Parents' Confusion

Whereas a decade ago, parents in my office and in my workshops cited real or imagined deficits in their children, now they utter vague complaints about their *own* impotence and confusion. This makes sense. Buried by an avalanche of childrearing how-to's over the last decade, parents today have become so anxious about doing the *wrong* thing that they are often paralyzed. They are not only failing to set limits for their kids, they sometimes don't even know what their *own* values are.

A key reason for parents' confusion is that over the last forty years, your average mother or father has been bombarded by a succession of one-size-fits-all childrearing techniques, which have swung crazily back and forth between the opposite poles of permissiveness and toughness. No wonder they're bewildered. Just as parents launch into the latest approach, they realize it has been supplanted by a new, often contradictory, tactic. For example, in the '70s parents willingly embraced Thomas Gordon's PET model—Parent Effectiveness Training. Antithetical to strict, Victorian childrearing theories, PET emphasized the importance of allowing children to express themselves freely and warned of psychological stultification if we suppressed a child's inner spirit. But a few years later, Tough Love followed hard on PET's heels; it emphasized limit-setting and quashed what was felt to be *too much* expressiveness. And so it went, through the decades. We saw the self-esteem movement come and go, along with family values and morality-based strategies, behavior modification, and medication. How can a parent *not* be confused about what's "right"?

The reality, which science bears out, is that no prepackaged program can possibly work. A review of the literature shows categorically that every child is an individual, not only different from other kids but from his or her own siblings as well. Over the last five years in particular, research has demonstrated an enormous variation in children's neurological makeup—their hard-wiring, if you will—which results in a wide range of temperamental and sensory differences. Some kids are mellower, some better at listening, some innately more cautious. What helps Johnny contain his aggression or concentrate more in school might easily fail with Bobby. And yet, decade after decade, we've been trying to come up with a singular "right" approach to childrearing. The bottom line is that parents, who tend to favor a particular technique, regardless of whether it is actually appropriate for their individual child, are left wanting.

For example, when her son Peter had gotten into another bruising battle with his little brother, Hillary employed PET. She tried to reason with Peter, by using Gordon's "active listening" techniques. She asked open-ended questions to help her sullen son express and neutralize his feelings of jealousy. The more she used this kind of dulcet-toned and carefully modulated therapy-speak, the more tight-lipped Peter became. Finally he looked at her in disgust and exclaimed, "Oh, forget it!" He walked away, leaving Mom speechless and feeling impotent.

Parenting strategies are not necessarily more effective at the authoritarian end of the continuum, as twelve-year-old Jenny's father found out. Jenny had been drinking, hooking up with lots of boys, staying out way past her curfew, and doing poorly in school. Her father, Bob, looking for a harder-line approach, was understandably attracted to Tough Love. He threatened Jenny with bottom-line consequences: "If you don't shape up, you're going to find yourself without a roof over your head." Before Dad could act on his hell-and-brimstone sermon, Jenny—of her own choosing—didn't come home at all, having found a place to crash with some loosely supervised kids in the neighborhood.

These are not uncommon stories—teenagers cursing at their parents, walking away, staying away from home, or simply looking at them like they're crazy. With most adults, teens tend to be coldly withdrawn, not obviously angry. This is different from the erratic behavior we've always expected from adolescents, where a young person blows up at her mother and then ten minutes later is sitting on her lap. These kids hardly ever waver. As one maddened parent put it, "There's not much we can do with him. He doesn't seem to care that we're upset. And no matter how we punish him, he doesn't flinch about the consequences." In the face of such attitudes, almost any off-the-rack approach, lenient or strict, is doomed to failure.

Too Few Rules and Too Much Relativism

The problem, though, is not just kids' intractability. Parents' plight is compounded by the fact that they abdicate their authority. I hear this from the children themselves: There aren't enough rules at home. Parents may threaten, "No TV for a week!" or they ground their kids. Still, mothers and fathers tend not to lay out consequences beforehand and rarely follow through on discipline. In part, this laissez faire attitude stems from the fact that many parents are skittish about being "in charge" of their kids. I suspect that the roots of this paradox date back to the '60s, when tradition was overturned and it became fashionable to distrust adults and to challenge authority. Coincidentally, many of the same baby boomers who spearheaded that movement are now parents, having trouble asserting their own parental authority.

"I don't want to quash his spirit," said one mother whose attitude is typical. "I'm not going to be a dictator like my own father," said a father. In Jared's case, his mother acknowledged that her son was "emotionally spoiled," but she quickly added that her permissiveness was, in part, her way of overcompensating, both for Jared's dad who spent many late nights at his law office, and her own guilt as well. Going back to work as a bank officer when Jared started kindergarten, Mom was acutely aware of "trying to make up for lost time." But the harder she tried to reach him, the more her son seemed to back away.

Such parents often bend over backward to ask kids' opinions, but they forget to express their own values. They tend to give their kids respect, but they don't demand respect in equal measure for themselves. To wit, when Melanie refused to buy her six-year-old son a toy in the supermarket, her little boy had a tantrum. She later reflected: "I didn't know whether it was better to smack him on the spot or let him get his feelings off his chest so they wouldn't fester."

Such a dilemma is intensified when a parent waffles over his or her own ethics. We're living in an age of moral relativism—a time when values are up for grabs. It's obvious that many parents have lost their direction. When ten-year-old Mindy was invited to a party where she knew kids would be making out, she asked her mom, Ann, "What should I do when they start kissing?" Mom was as unsure as her little girl. After hesitating, she told her daughter, "In the end, it's what makes *you* feel comfortable with who you are." Ann later confided in me that she didn't know what would be better, letting Mindy "harmlessly" explore her emerging sexuality or setting strict limits that she might rebel against—and risking Mindy's choosing not to confide in her next time.

If moral values are on a sliding scale, and once immutable concepts like "good" and "bad" and "right" and "wrong" are called into question, that means that each situation must be weighed for its own merits. Neither parents, nor teachers, and certainly not therapists, feel comfortable imposing their values. Hence, when Kris, age five, was called "out" at a Little League game, though she ran up to the umpire, shouted, "I hate you!" and proceeded to kick him in the shins three times, no one called her on it. Her admittedly embarrassed mother didn't so much as reprimand her, nor did the umpire feel right throwing Kris out of the game. In fact, a few minutes later, Kris was given the weekly achievement badge she had "earned" simply by showing up to play.

Teen Credo: Live and Let Live

If Kris is like the younger children in my study, she is already aware that something is wrong with this picture and doesn't like it. Up to age eight or nine, kids tell me they wish that their parents would be more directive, offering them real rules not rubbery ones. By fourth or fifth grade, though, Kris could begin to change, becoming more like the older children in my studies who are just as happy to make their own rules. Apt pupils of moral relativism, they're comfortable on the slippery slope of good and bad. By then, they're sufficiently involved with the second family to have adopted its dominating ethos: *live and let live*.

This can be seen in national studies of teen attitudes as well. When adolescents in the heartland of America were asked by the *Rockford Star Register* about their own moral guidelines, the Illinois youth answered almost unanimously: "There aren't any. You only need to treat others the same way they treat you." Almost none of these teenagers, boys *or* girls, were prepared to label any behavior, no matter how noxious, as simply right or wrong. Even more disquieting is that few of these kids had ever considered that adults might in some way be able to guide them in making decisions about moral issues. And why should these kids think so? Most of the grown-ups in their lives don't believe in their own ability to redirect their children, nor do they understand what it's like to be an adolescent today—a failure kids pick up on all too well.

So what happens to so many children today when they do not get the kind of direct, undivided, personal attention they need from their own parents? Where do they look to find something that promises to assuage their yearning for attention? Their hunger for ritual? To whom do they turn when they realize that the adults in their life lack the confidence to guide them and the strength to rein them in? They find their own way—right into the arms of the second family. The second family offers not only excitement and instant gratification, but also the personal comfort that comes with a sense of identity, belonging, and rituals—a role that was once the province of the first family at home.

Nature abhors a vacuum, and over the last decade the great, roaring hurricane of the kid-centered mass media culture has rushed in to fill the psychic void that beleaguered, bewildered parents have unwittingly created. Today, companies producing everything from backpacks to bed linens know full well that most kids will choose a *Pokémon* T-shirt over one without a recognizable image. We buy these products for our kids, put computers in their rooms, and take them to the latest movies, because we don't want them to feel like outsiders or to miss out on what all the other kids are doing and talking about. But even if we didn't aid and abet the pop culture, thanks to the explosion in technology, the advertisements and artifacts would still flow into our homes.

Suddenly, all children, literally all over the world, are talking the same language, vying for the same toys, playing the same games, watching the same programs on TV. They have exclusive entry to Planet Youth, and we are not invited. By the time these kids reach adolescence, they have spun out of our control, and they are not like any teenagers we've ever encountered.

The New Adolescent Anger

Classic adolescent rebellion has always been about separating, first and foremost, from one's parents. But teens nowadays already feel separate from their parents. There isn't an oppressive parent blocking their way to the front door, demanding, "Where are you going?" More often, a parent is shooing them out the door saying, "It's four o'clock—time to leave for your art class." In essence, we've pushed our kids out of the nest, and now we're living with the consequence: separate worlds. We're off somewhere, fretting over jobs and finances, figuring out how to have meaningful relationships. We worry about our children, too, but they're already in an orbit of their own choosing. If they're angry at all, it's not because we're babying them or holding them back. It's because they don't feel held in their own families.

But make no mistake: The kids I speak with are not necessarily down on their parents. For example, when I first met Bryan, who ended up in my office after setting fire to a wastebasket in his school, I assumed that he was angry at mom and dad. Suggesting as much, I heard, "What do my parents have to do with it?" In actuality, Bryan admired his father, a successful merchant, for the money he made and for his openness. He felt that his mother, a personnel administrator, nagged him a little too much, but it was obvious that he really loved her and thought highly of her accomplishments, too. In old-think terms, Bryan's vandalism appeared to be an angry act, directed at all the adults in his life, not just his parents. But seen through the prism of new-think, he was motivated more by detachment, and a feeling of emptiness, than discontent.

Rarely do teens nowadays make disdainful declarations such as, "I never want to be like my mother/father" — a mantra in past generations. The most common criticism I hear is, "They don't have a clue." Brian spoke for many of the kids I've encountered when he remarked dolefully: "My parents don't know me."

Fourteen-year-old Carter felt the same way. To the shock and humiliation of his parents, he had thrown a party for three hundred kids when they were out of town tending to his *dying grandmother*. He casually explained his motive to his absolutely devastated mother: "I thought it would be fun." At the time still handicapped by my old-think mind, I probed further, sure that there was some deep, underlying resentment.

"Isn't it possible that you are also saying something against *your parents*?" I asked gently. His brain simply couldn't compute this. "Are you saying you think I'm angry at them?" he countered, a look of bewilderment on his face.

The point is, teens like these aren't coming into my office with chronic complaints about their parents. Nor are they riddled with guilt over their own behavior. Sure, kids have always lied to adults, but these children are better at it, rarely conflicted or afraid of the consequences. They are glib, but not proud, about their ability to "get over" on adults. I'd go so far to say that most actually present like "nice" kids — unlike what I once expected from adolescents, there is rarely a "fuck you" underlying their actions.

The truth is, we can no longer interpret teenage aggression as rage against parents or even society. Nor are these acts a matter of kids "snapping" and their anger getting the best of them. Rather, *these are kids who are desperate to be seen.* What could be more public than the kinds of scandalous behavior I've described: Sex in the bathroom in school or the back of the bus? Vandalism of public buildings? Teens involved in daring, dangerous exploits like jumping off a bridge? These are all outrageous acts—blatant attempts at becoming known.

The Modern Cult of Celebrity

A grisly confirmation of this new adolescent mentality unfolded in the last days of the millennium, with the release of what has become known as "the Columbine tapes"—a series of videos made by teen killers Dylan Klebold and Eric Harris in the weeks prior to their April 20, 1999, massacre of thirteen students and teachers. When the shooting first happened, parents, police, and assorted social observers put forth the old theories: the boys were loners, teased by the jocks and popular kids, and their anger finally got the best of them. Wrong. "It turns out there is much more to the story than that," reported *Time* magazine months later, after the tapes were finally released. The lead story purported that "retaliation against specific people was not the point" and that the horrific event "may have been about celebrity as much as cruelty."

Just as I have seen in my practice, there was no evidence in the tapes that these boys were raging at their parents. On the contrary, *Time* noted, "Throughout the videotapes, it seems as though the only people about whom the killers felt remorse were their parents. 'It f——ing sucks to do this to them,' Harris says of his parents. 'They're going to be put through hell once we do this.' " On the tapes, both boys appeal directly to their parents. Harris seems to be trying to ease his mother and father's burden: "There's nothing you guys could've done to prevent this." And Klebold tells his mom and dad that they were "great parents" who taught him "self-awareness, self-reliance . . . I always appreciated that." He adds, "I'm sorry I have so much rage."

Listening to the tapes, *Time* concluded, "It is clear that Harris and Klebold were not just having trouble with what their counselors called 'anger management.' They fed the anger, fueled it, so the fury could take hold, because they knew they would need it to do what they had set out to do." In other words, anger was not some amorphous force that took hold of these teens and caused them to spin out of control. Rather, it was a tool that they used to deal with their desperate need to be known. They plotted consciously, drawing strength from their rage. Mass murder was the terrible and deliberate end, not simply a by-product of anger.

To be sure, the Columbine tragedy is an extreme example of teenage alienation and angst gone awry. But I hear the same underlying story in many of the kids I see—kids whose infractions are far less serious. In a culture where so many forces compete for adults' eyes and ears, children like Bryan, who vandalize school property, rarely have their parents' undivided attention. Often, neither their mothers nor their fathers know much about their interests. Kids just want to go to a place where they can hang out and be appreciated for who they are. And there is such a place—the second family—which offers children not only a sense of being known, but also the promise of celebrity.

In a sense, *celebrities are the priests of the second family,* and its members long to touch their vestments, thereby conferring onto themselves some small degree of recognition. The pop culture shows kids that it is possible to literally make a name for yourself. Teens, weaned on second-family values, understand the process, because they watch it unfold with the overnight fame of each new youthful media icon—the street kids who become rap stars, the athletes who make more money playing in one game than most adults earn in a year, the twentysomething Internet whizzes who become instant millionaires. *If kids can't get undivided acknowledgment at home, if their parents fail to notice their uniqueness, the pop culture teaches them that it's possible to become known by other means.*

I see this phenomenon in varying degrees of intensity. Ordinary kids find recognition in peer groups. They take solace in the fact that their friends know them and that they have found a place in their clique. The more desperate—the children who are hungrier for acknowledgment—need more. They must distinguish themselves by becoming the school bully, the class clown, the dark dropout, the dangerous druggie, the violent vandal. And the most despairing and dangerous teens find that their school and even their community are not enough. Those truly on the fringe, like Klebold and Harris, want *the world* to know them—dead *or* alive.

That these two young men from good, middle-class families specifically made those videotapes detailing their macabre plan exemplifies this cult of celebrity—albeit its most extreme and frightening manifestation. Like most teenagers, Klebold and Harris had seen miles of television footage broadcasting savage acts. They understood the power of cinema verité from offerings like *Cops*, and MTV's *Real World* and *Road Rules*. They knew full well that they were staging a media event, knew that producers like Quentin Tarantino would be "fighting over this story," and knew that talking heads throughout the world would be desperate to understand their acts. These boys were not merely drawn into the second family—they were deeply entrenched. "You have two individuals who wanted to immortalize themselves," FBI agent Mark Holstlaw is quoted in *Time* magazine.

To be sure, we're living in frightening, unprecedented times. Society is composed of fragmented families, with parents and children living parallel lives. It is a world in which children often feel more catered to than truly known, where off-the-rack childrearing techniques complicate more than they resolve, and where moral relativism is the norm. In such a milieu, the cult of celebrity is the potentially flammable ingredient. *Kids who commit publicly violent or outrageous acts have found the metaphor that describes the pain of, as well as the solution for, their invisibility. Such behavior makes an unknown child instantly and uniquely recognizable. In a child's mind, this is the perfect antidote for the anonymity of his or her life.*

What Can Adults Do?

Over the last few years, as the public watched the horror of the many schoolyard shootings unfold, everyone began to point fingers at the parents. "Where were their mothers and fathers?" ask the teachers, the guidance counselors, coaches, the other parents (thanking their lucky stars it wasn't *their* teenager who got into serious trouble). Some parents take the blame upon themselves. Like Jared's mother and father, each criticizes what the other has or has not done. Dad's always at the office or on the road; Mom dotes on the child too much and doesn't allow him to grow up. But what neither parents nor the professionals who advise them—even some family therapists—don't realize is that they're all swimming in the same cultural seas. It's no one's fault; it's just what is.

In some respects, today's adults are faced with the same dilemma as the immigrants who came here in the first half of the century—my own parents, for example, who emigrated from Europe in 1939. They, too, were stymied by the behavior of their first-generation American children. Despite wanting the best opportunities for us—benefits that only living in the United States would bring—they, too, stood by helpless and confused as their children assimilated into a culture that was alien to everything the older generation held dear. They barely understood their kids' language, no less the fashions, the music, and the activities they fancied. The difference was that back then the pop culture didn't loom quite as large. Sure, we had Davy Crockett hats and hula hoops, but nothing even close to the kind of merchandising efforts we see now. Moreover, although much pain existed behind closed doors, there were powerful extended families and involved adults in communities. Sometimes they offered parents solace and support and, even more important, were there to help keep kids in line.

For better or worse, no such lifeline exists today. But we can't just throw our hands up and lament the far-reaching changes in society that have left adults isolated and confused. Nor can we simply blame the schools or the media and criticize the commercialization of childhood. We also have to look at what's happened *inside* the first family at home to understand why our kids are so susceptible to the lure of the second family.

Kids frequently say to me, "My parents don't have a clue." They're right. In fact, most adults don't understand what kids get from the second family, or why they're so connected to it. However, the fact that many parents and other adults who deal with teenagers lack this "insider" knowledge of Planet Youth means there's a lot we adults *can* do.

To increase our understanding of what kids today are like and what they're really dealing with, we can't cling to old beliefs. It is simply no longer true, for example, that kids get into trouble primarily because of "peer pressure." We must grasp the important fact that, for better or worse, the second family operates just like other types of families, with a well-defined internal structure and explicit values and rules of its own. By understanding precisely how and why our kids become so involved in the second family and by deciphering its rules of membership, all adults who deal with children can learn what kids want from us and how we need to act toward them. Hence, in the next chapter I will look *inside* the second family, and, in doing so, let you see how it can teach us ways to reach out for and stay connected to our kids.

2

"You Adults Don't Have a Clue"

Understanding the Second Family

Adolescence is not what most of us think it is. It's happening at earlier ages and teens are seeking comfort as much as a sense of identity. When we try to apply timeworn theories, it only confirms kids' notion that we have no idea. Hence, to understand the developmental process by which a child becomes immersed in the second family, we must be prepared to open our eyes and relinquish our old beliefs.

Truths and Misconceptions

When fifteen-year-old Jason, a student in a Boston suburb, was caught playing poker for money and threatened with expulsion, his parents, Helen and Richard, concluded, "He's in with a bad crowd." They were sure that their son's impulsive behavior, which also included drinking and minor incidents of vandalism, was the result of hanging out with a group of slackers whom he'd met while skateboarding. Jason had been spending just about every waking minute with those kids, Richard explained. "Certainly, he has a mind of his own, but I also know what peer pressure can do."

Case after case, I hear a similar refrain from parents: their child is getting into trouble because of another kid's bad influence. When parents blame a teen's misbehavior on peer pressure, it's partly a matter of self-defense and denial: *my* child wouldn't smoke pot or take risks unless he were goaded into it—he's certainly no ring leader. But it's partly tradition, too. Most adults cling to the timeworn conviction that when a kid gets into trouble it's because his friends led him down the primrose path. They believe that some nefarious Svengali-like character steps out of the shadows to offer killer weed. Or, the class troublemaker threatens, dares, or demands as a show of allegiance that everyone else follow his example: "Smoke this cigarette or you're a pussy." "Shoplift with me or you're out of the group." And the weak kids, the ones who desperately want to be liked, follow blindly.

It's not only parents who imagine such scenes. I, too, fell prey to the same kind of outmoded reasoning. After all, the stock explanation — kids will follow what others do because they don't want to risk being ostracized — has been applied to troubled adolescents since the '50s. From time immemorial, adults have served up admonishments such as "I know you'll feel pressured to drink if I let you go to Mary's party," or "Don't hang out with Dirk, because he's a troublemaker." So it's only natural that, as a therapist, I'd take a similar tack. But kids today are not merely astounded by such comments, they often have no idea what we're talking about.

"Do my parents think I'm *that* weak or stupid?" Jason snapped angrily, when I innocently echoed his parent's theories about his recent troubles.

Naturally, teachers and counselors, who try in vain to connect with young people, often labor under the same misconception, too. For example, Mrs. Daley, attempting to prepare a group of preteens to withstand the strains of early dating, sat the seventh-grade girls down and gently warned that boys might try to "pressure" them. Date rape, she (correctly) cautioned, was all too common. The girls in the room — among them Olivia, a twelve-year-old I know — looked at each other, wisecracked a bit, and resumed doodling in their notebooks.

"I'm sure it happens, but I don't personally know any girl who feels forced," protested Olivia, later relating to me the content of Mrs. Daley's heart-to-heart discussion. "With most of my friends, that's just not the way it works."

Indeed it isn't.

Understanding Teens' Reality

Modern teenagers' motivation is different from what most of us once believed and continue to expect. As hard as this is for parents to accept, when a kid gets involved with alcohol, illicit substances, or other adult fare, in most cases it is *not*, as old-think would have us believe, because of coercion by peers. A phenomenon that I call the *tyranny of cool* (see page 44) can be a factor in *younger* teens' motivation and behavior, but by mid-adolescence, most kids feel little pressure to conform.

Another classic view of adolescence also highlights teens' need for separation, the search for a sense of self. Therefore, we tend to chalk up teen back talk, distancing, lies, and other misdeeds to teenage rebellion. Wrong again. It's true that today's teens are also searching for an identity, but their primary impetus is *comfort*.

As always, it was kids themselves who helped me change my perspective. In a conversation with three fourteen-year-old boys about curfews, I saw how easy it was to reach the wrong conclusion about teenagers' motives. One of the boys, Seth, had gotten into trouble because he had stayed out past his curfew. I assumed that Seth's parents were overly strict. Gavin and Peter were probably allowed to stay out later than him. I figured that Seth, wanting to keep up with his buddies, therefore ignored his own curfew. I was dead wrong on all counts.

Peter's curfew *was* later—eleven-thirty. But it was Gavin, not Seth, who had to be in earlier than the others. Seeing that it was nearing ten, Gavin dutifully left the video arcade at 9:45. His friends were "cool" with it, as Seth explained matter-of-factly. "His parents are like that. It has nothing to do with what we think of Gavin—he just has to live by a different set of rules." In reality, Seth's missing his own curfew had little to do with his wanting to be like Peter or anger toward his parents' rules, which he actually thought were quite fair. He was simply comfortable where he was, didn't feel like leaving, and, in the process, lost track of time.

I hear this theme of reflexively seeking one's comfort level in many of my sessions with kids. With Elliott, for example, I was trying to figure out why this kid was such a chronically "lazy slacker," to use his own words. To gain insight, I invited Elliott to bring his friend Mary with him. The two had grown up together — their mothers were high school friends — and they were still in the same school, now in seventh grade.

"Why do you think Elliott isn't such a hard worker?" I asked Mary, who was herself an A student.

"I've thought about it," Mary said, "He's not into school. It's just not his thing." She accepted that studying didn't figure into Elliot's comfort level. No judgment, perhaps slight worry, but absolutely no desire to reform her friend.

The Death of Peer Pressure

As I stressed in Chapter One, the fundamental ethos of the second family is *live and let live.* Peer pressure, as we knew it even ten years ago, is essentially dead. Difficult as this may be for adults to grasp, kids don't particularly try to influence each other. More to the point, many teens are proud that whether it's a case of cheating on a test, lying to parents, goofing off in school, disregarding curfews, smoking dope, having sex, or any other exploits that rightfully concern adults, teens neither feel compelled to imitate the behavior of nor cast judgment on kids who do.

I am sometimes taken aback by this attitude. Monica, a girl I'd been counseling, told me in a rather nonchalant way that she had cautioned one of her friends about the dangers of selling drugs in school. Then she added a comment I've increasingly come to expect from adolescents in this new-world order: "I had to say it in a way that Gail didn't feel like I was pushing my attitude on her."

I also remember the day I tried to prepare fourteen-year-old Liam for a concert that he had been begging his parents to attend. Liam had done his share of pot-smoking in seventh and eighth grade but was now trying to "lay off weed," as he put it.

Hearing this, I gave him the old rap: "Won't it be hard for you to resist taking a joint if someone else offers you one at the concert?"

Liam looked at me like I was crazy. *What world was I from?* "No one is going to force me," he answered as if it were obvious, "or make me feel bad for not doing it. My friends don't think I'm any less cool now that I'm not smoking—they could care less." He was also quite clear on another point: "No one pushed me to smoke in the first place."

Sure, very young adolescents will still say, "I wish I were more like Tommy. He's king of the world," but it's rarely a matter of Tommy coercing the younger kid into mischief. Children, of course, want to belong, and the second family does a great job of providing a haven for them. However, in our increasingly broad-minded culture, belonging doesn't mean imposing one's values on anyone else. For one thing, teenagers already have such strong bonds with their peers they have no need to feel the kind of solidarity that comes with mob rule and common misdeeds. I know this goes against every old-think rule we've heard, but the truth is, *if a budding adolescent doesn't want to try a glass of beer or smoke a joint, no one is going to force him or her.*

The way we used to think about peer pressure is also invalid because, as I pointed out in the Prologue, teenagers mirror attitudes that prevail in the grownup world. A recent Gallup poll showed that the vast majority of adults believe that how one worships or what one does in private is entirely up to that person. The public's widespread refusal to judge Bill Clinton's indiscretions exemplifies this mentality of moral relativism: as long as you're not in my face, and you're not hurting me or someone I love, you can do what you like and follow whatever credo works for you.

Kids have learned these lessons well. As fifteen-year-old Trevor said of his girlfriend, Lea, who had decided to spend New Year's Eve with a girlfriend instead of him, "I'm not going to force my beliefs on her." Sure, Trevor was upset—he would have liked to spend the evening with Lea. But when she explained that she had long ago made this promise to Marcy, her best friend, he sighed. "That's what she thinks is right."

I hear stories like this from the hundreds of kids I've interviewed and those I see in my practice. And yet the adults in their lives continue to dole out the old platitudes—"Just say no!" "Think for yourself," "Stick with the good kids," "Don't do something just because others are doing it." Such statements are yet another bit of proof for teens that just about all adults, not only their parents, don't really have a clue about who they are—or where their ideas about life are coming from.

The Myth of Sex, Drugs, Rock 'n' Roll

Another gross misconception is that kids use alcohol and sex to protest the adult order. That equation is backward. Nowadays when kids get into such activities, it's rarely out of rebellion. Most often, it's simply because those illicit temptations are readily available to them from the "fun" menu of life. In point of fact, activities in which previous generations indulged only by getting involved with a bad crowd and peeking into the forbidden adult universe are now part of *their* world. Drugs, sex, and rock 'n' roll are, like a Visa card, everywhere a kid wants to be.

To wit, fifteen-year-old Adam's quick and disarmingly honest answer when I asked his advice about keeping pornography out of my house: "Oh, you could put parental controls on your TV, and that may buy you some time, but it won't make any difference in the long run. Your kids will see porno on TV or a video or in a magazine at someone else's house. Besides," Adam added nonchalantly, "it's not such a big deal. We've all seen it . . . and so will they."

Adam has a point. Children today are uncannily precocious about sexual matters, and it's due to the explicit content of routine pop culture fare. Where previous generations had to sneak books off their parents' bookshelves to learn the mysteries of sex, these kids have grown up with graphic sexual content—on TV shows, in music videos, and in movies. Children can tune into a "blue channel" on TV or log on to X-rated Internet sites; and, together, they can figure out ways of circumventing parents' intrusion. They become savvy consumers of the double entendre, absorbing the quick patter of sitcoms like *Friends*. Nine Inch Nails' hit song "Starfuckers" needs no translation for the MTV generation. Song lyrics teach them the details of sexual acts—for instance, Allanis Morissette singing about oral sex: "wine dine 69 me." So, when they see a sexy young thing dropping to her knees in front of the Dawson character on *Dawson's Creek*, and the camera highlights Dawson's enraptured face, even preteen viewers, who comprise a large number of the audience, knew just what the scene implied.

Children who have grown up with the language of sex talk precociously and openly about the most intimate matters. Granted, sex has always been on teens' minds, but the banter has never crossed gender lines quite so easily. It's not uncommon to hear boys in the playground making wisecracks to girls about their "boobs" and "tits." They may accuse a girl of "having her period" or "PMS-ing." In some schools, such heckling is labeled harassment. Administrators and teachers try to develop policies about how to prevent it and what girls should say in response, but it's proving nearly impossible to get kids to act differently.

I hasten to add, modern girls are far from defenseless in the arena of verbal harassment. It's not that teenage girls aren't taken advantage of by boys or that date rape doesn't exist, but many of them are amazingly deft at slinging back insults that would appall their parents: Taunted by one of her older brother's friends, a seven-year-old mutters "penis breath." An eleven-year-old girl, annoyed by a boy, shouts across the yard, "I hope your dick is bigger than your brain."

Drugs and alcohol are ubiquitous, too. Liquor flows at parties hosted by the best and the brightest. Most kids don't even need to leave home to imbibe. In many cities and some suburban areas as well, teens tell me it's possible to "order in" pot. Some dealers hand out business cards, offer a menu of different varieties, and promise delivery in under thirty minutes — faster than Domino's. Kids also boast of "borrowing" from a parent's "stash" or harvesting leaves from a home-grown plant. Perry, a teenager I know, tells me that nowadays pot is so prevalent in public venues — movies, theaters, arenas — that, "If routine drug tests were administered after concerts, we'd all fail, even kids who never took a toke."

Ironically, some of the very steps adults have taken to protect kids actually provide them with easy access to both counterculture know-how and substances. For example, many schools today have instituted buddy systems, whereby older students are assigned to younger ones, allegedly to help them get acclimated. When not closely monitored, the older ones do, in fact, show their younger counterparts the ropes, but the lessons are not always what the PTA has in mind: what products to use to bleach your hair, the best places for body piercing, how to score pot and hold your liquor. A similar indoctrination happens in unsupervised afternoon gatherings at kids' houses, when an older sibling takes the younger kids under her wing, even at summer camps when a counselor says to his wards, "Wanna try some?"

Increasingly, I've found in my family interviews that older brothers and sisters are the first to introduce their siblings to some of the pleasures and dangers of the second family. It has become commonplace for me to hear stories like Cynthia's. As a junior in high school, she ushered her younger brother, Mark, through his first pot-smoking experience while their parents were away for the weekend. Cynthia believed there was nothing wrong about her extracurricular activities with Mark. As she put it, "Since it's gonna happen anyway, he might as well have his first experience with someone who loves him."

Millennium siblings don't believe in a double standard; it wouldn't even occur to most older brothers that they should "protect" a sister from drugs or sex. Matt, for example, actually covered for his younger sister's first sexual experiences by making sure Mom and Dad were distracted when they tried to extract details of Sally's whereabouts and activities. Just like many second-family kids, Matt believes what he thinks is obvious: "What makes my parents think they're gonna be able to stop Sally anyway?"

As you will read throughout this book, teens zealously guard their privacy and their independence. They close ranks when it comes to adults, protecting each other against prying adults *within* the family. Even if older siblings haven't actually introduced their younger brothers or sisters to drugs, informed or abetted their sexual experimentation, they certainly know about each other's second-family activities but will rarely share that information with their parents. If a child is in severe danger, they might, but otherwise the live-and-let-live credo prevails. As several female college freshmen told me in interviews, "Yeah, I know my brothers are smoking a lot of dope, but it's not for me to tell them what to do."

The bottom line is it's all out there for today's teens and increasingly preteens: a bouquet of fun, temptations, and dangers. There for the picking because it's simply part of the pop culture, which your child and mine have been a part of since early childhood. Nothing is off-limits. And because of the peer network's instant communication, tricks of the trade are easily and quickly disseminated, almost always without adults' knowledge.

A Culture of Comfort

If teenagers' involvement in sex, drugs, and other pop culture attractions isn't about eating forbidden fruit, if it isn't about rebellion, and if it isn't about peer pressure, then what *is* the reason they become so immersed in and devoted to the second family? The surprising key is not just the obvious—belonging—but, more important, *comfort*. By adolescence, each child finds within this closed system, not only a home, but a cozy, relaxed sense of identity.

It starts with the very young, who are sucked into the powerful vortex of the second family almost from birth, when their little eyes fix on Muppet Baby crib bumpers and Mickey Mouse mobiles. Admittedly, the process is both subtle and gradual—a developmental continuum, if you will. Kids move through three levels: *Introduction*, where they become oriented; *Exploration*, where they begin to develop personal tastes and values; and, finally, *Comfort*, where they truly settle in. Watching this progression we see an escalating pattern: the more a child moves toward the *Comfort* end of the continuum, the less he or she wants to be involved in first-family life at home.

Indeed, there's a generation of kids out there devoted to media and merchandising, dependent mostly on their peers for guidance, and, in the worst sense, divorced from their parents and other adults. In varying degrees, I see the evidence everywhere, with my kids, in the homes of friends, in the schools I visit. Within minutes of meeting a child, I can tell where he or she falls on the continuum.

This point bears repeating: second-family involvement is *not* limited to kids who are poor students or those on the fringe who have social and psychological problems. Those children are undoubtedly most vulnerable; they typically have histories of chronically poor performance in school and tend to move on to more serious trouble—drugs, sexual acting out, gambling, or vandalism. But virtually *every* child today is affected by the pull of the second family—boys *and* girls, whether economically privileged or deprived, from divorced or intact families, with working or stay-at-home moms, absentee or involved fathers.

The second family is a force of modern life that's here to stay and unless you happen to be living in some extreme outpost of rural America, don't have a computer, your child is home-schooled and sees few other kids, or watches no TV, it's virtually impossible for a youngster growing up in America today not to be touched. We adults, to put it in kids' vernacular, simply have to "deal." We can't ignore the second family, stop its influence, or wish it away. What we can do is be aware of its power and guide our kids down a less destructive path.

Understanding is the key to reclaiming our kids.

Spanning the Continuum

As they age, kids move through the three loosely defined levels of escalating second-family involvement: *Introduction*, *Exploration*, and *Comfort*. Although parents may not know or use the term *second family*, their kids are somewhere on the continuum. Mothers and fathers find themselves baffled and a little tickled at the *Introduction* level, amazed by their three-year-old's uncanny knowledge of the pop culture. They are frustrated and even resentful at the *experimental* level, sensing that something or someone is beginning to pull their third-grader away from them. And they become understandably frightened at the *comfort* level, impotently watching as their preteen slips progressively farther from them, contentedly making a new home for himself on Planet Youth. Looking for the signposts of each level, it's fairly easy to determine just how far a child has traveled along the continuum.

Introduction. We unwittingly induct our kids into the pop culture when we plop them in front of the TV, buy them their first media-inspired stuffed animal, or read them a book based on a TV show or movie. As evidenced by a number of studies about television programs, the process starts at younger and younger ages. For reasons I've already outlined, among them our desire to "enrich" and the fact that parents are so busy, we actually sanction most of these early second-family pursuits — network and cable TV, video games, dinners at the local fast-food restaurant, trips to media-subsidized theme parks and vacation venues. All these activities have come to be a part of everyday family life — often, a really enjoyable part.

As children watch the movies, play the games, and clamor for the toys, they're absorbing the values of the second family. They quickly become one with the media. A friend of mine was horrified when her four-month-old granddaughter, sitting in an infant seat in front of the TV, held out her chubby little arms to the flickering images of *Sesame Street's* Big Bird. "I had yet to see her make a gesture like that toward her parents!" A similar phenomenon was highlighted in a *Simpsons* episode, in which older siblings Bart and Lisa are vying for baby Maggie's affection. "Who do you choose?" each demands. Maggie, barely pausing, runs to the TV and hugs it, thereby declaring her true allegiance. The mythical Maggie is probably around two, the age that many children first become susceptible to second-family lures. Huge numbers of little ones are already humming advertising jingles or vigorously lobbying for a trip to a particular fast-food restaurant because they want the giveaways offered this week.

Moreover, because increasing numbers of children enter day care and nursery school, in a sense they are "leaving home" earlier than ever and, most important, developing peer-group connections at younger ages than they once did. It is here that the die is cast. From the time they're six months old, children begin relating extensively to other children. They play together; they watch television and videos together. (A recent study found that in 70 percent of day-care centers, television is used at least part of the time.) Thus, even for kids this young, powerful and lasting relationships are forged with *peers* who often travel with them from preschool through high school — not with adult caregivers, such as teachers, counselors, and coaches, who typically change from year to year. This first alternate "family" of day care is actually the earliest form of the second family — a foreshadowing of things to come. Even as their kids age, parents drop them off—to birthday parties, child-centered play groups, and commercial play zones. Relatively few adults are present.

This strict division between the adult and child world is, in part, an economic necessity when both parents work. But it is also a by-product of psychological theories and practices that blossomed after World War II, advancing the notion that for optimal learning to take place, activities and classes for children ought to be developmentally appropriate. Today, within the entire child world, virtually everything is stratified according to age. Toys are developmentally specific. TV programs and movies are aimed at a fairly narrow age group, too. Even kid entertainers seek an age-specific niche. A clown makes the round of four-year-olds' birthday parties; a balloon sculptor specializes in six-year-olds; a science magician becomes the darling of the eight-year-old set.

Thus, youngsters are subtly programmed to think that they can relate only to their peers. Three-year-olds are in play groups with three-year-olds; later, as seventh-graders, it will make total sense to them that they play baseball only with other seventh-graders. In and of itself, grouping kids by age isn't bad. Nor are the child-centered activities and products inherently harmful—many, in fact, do reinforce skills and foster kids' creativity. And, competent and affordable day care has certainly been a boon to working parents, so we shouldn't turn back the clock there. The problem is, this separate-worlds mentality subtly relegates parents to the sidelines of their children's lives. And as children are pulled deeper and deeper into the second-family interests, not only parents, but all adults, pale by comparison.

Exploration. Moving into the elementary school years, typically grades one through grades five or six, children embrace catchphrases such as "Nickelodeon Nation" and that channel's motto, "Kids rule!," which crystallize the ethos of their child-centered universe. The media has become a main reference point, the "gimmees" are in high gear, and peers are starting to gain prominence over parents. In my parent workshops, I hear about seven-year-olds who clamor for the "hottest" movies, video games, toys, and fashions; eight-year-olds who communicate via phone and E-mail; nine-year-olds who subscribe to "fanzines."

These kids form a solid connection that adults can't totally understand or completely penetrate. Watching sitcoms and listening to TV characters' wisecracks, they grasp the media-generated notion that parents are people with whom you must negotiate to get "stuff" and privileges. Many of these programs and commercials actually teach kids how to wrangle with adults—behavior that used to be the province of teens. Now younger and younger kids are testing these waters.

By the *Exploration* level, we also see what I call *the tyranny of cool*, a phenomenon once associated solely with teenagers. During the mid- to late-elementary years, popularity becomes the primary currency of the second family, and at this level "nerdphobia" begins to dominate a kid's life. These children—who are in elementary to middle school, not high school—quickly grasp which sneakers, which backpack, even which kind of sandwich in their lunch box earns the respect of their peers. In their admittedly short lifetime, children at the *Exploration* level have seen thousands of cleverly crafted thirty-second commercials, repeatedly promoting the idea that satisfaction and self-worth come from the outside, with the acquisition of material goods. Accordingly, the competition is fierce, for who has the most, the best, the coolest. I was not surprised when a little girl in a shoe store, probably no older than six, said to her mother, "Not those, Mom. They're cute, but they're not cool." Nor did it shock me that in one school I visited, the third-grade girls categorized their male classmates as either "nerds" or "boy-boys." When I asked them to explain what "boy-boys" were, one told me, "The *real* boys. They dress right, they walk and talk right—they're cool!"

The second family also values watching over doing, fun over responsibility, and it's hard for children to resist its lure. Therefore, although children at the *Exploration* level are busy making their way up the pecking order as they're trying out new activities and ideas, they're starting to become more invested in having a good time—being comfortable. This is juxtaposed with the increasingly hard work that's now expected of them. It's no accident that these are the grades during which school problems first begin to crop up. By fourth grade, when schoolwork becomes harder and more demanding, many children are already enamored of the nondemanding world of the second family, preferring its alternative reality over the difficulties of real life. Their peers don't expect much of them, and, unlike what happens at home or at school, this is a universe they can control. Kids are able to choose the most comfortable level of difficulty on their video games, and switch the channel or visit a different Internet site whenever they're restless. Not surprisingly, second-family devotees are unable to stick with boring chores or repetitive tasks, which is why many have trouble when it comes to early reading skills and other academic undertakings. Such children balk at participating in things that don't provide instant gratification or, worse, activities that require work, practice, or the frustration of being a beginner.

Comfort. By this time, typically the end of sixth grade or the beginning of seventh, we see kids so deeply enmeshed in second-family values and pursuits that they're drawn only to that which promises immediate reward for very little effort. At this level, media-consumed children begin dropping out of after-school clubs and teams. The once-promising gymnast doesn't want to practice anymore. The precociously astute chess player now says the game is too boring. The kid with a great arm decides there are "too many regulations" in Little League. If an activity is preferred, often it's one the second family condones—that is, anything with few rules, fewer adults, and little pressure to perform. Boys turn to skateboarding, in-line skating, or other x-treme sports that involve risk and minimal restrictions. Their musical tastes often run to heavy metal or rap, the style is grunge or gansta. Girls go in for teen-fashion extremes, from preppie to goth—which may involve neon hair-dying and multiple body-piercing, tattooing, fad dieting, and, of course, high-tech celebrity fervor. Girls regularly log on to Web sites tailored to their age group, devour the exponentially increasing number of early adolescent entertainment magazines, and see their favorite movies over and over, which accounts for the huge box-office grosses of contemporary teen-sanctioned films.

Adults are nonentities to true second-family disciples. In fact, these teens are sick of grownups, which is another reason for their high drop-out rate from extracurricular activities. By the time boys and girls reach the *Comfort* level, they've had their fill of scheduled guardians. Farmed out by busy parents since infancy, these kids have been in day care and in preschool programs, like Baby Guppies and Gymboree, and, later, in various clubs, teams, and after-school groups—all of which were run by professional kid wranglers who were paid to teach, encourage, amuse, or monitor them. Because most programs last eight weeks, a semester, or a year at most, young people never really spend enough time with any single adult to develop meaningful allegiances or mentoring relationships. So what's the constant in their lives? Certainly not parents or grandparents, nor the parade of transient adults that marched through their childhood. No, these kids look to their *peers* for guidance and support—peers who don't criticize or correct but merely accept them for who they are.

In their live-and-let-live worlds, friends don't demand much. When I ask Jared, in his baggy pants and torn T-shirt, a typical pop-culture-saturated teen, "What's so great about being with your friends?" he has a ready answer.

"I don't have to *do* anything. I don't have to be good at anything. There's no pressure."

Understandably, when teens have reached this far end of the continuum—typically by junior or senior high—the second family all but replaces the first. These adolescents have a huge, supportive network of friends who think just like them, act like them, don't care about school, and view their parents from the same distant perspective. Everything is colored by second-family thinking. And thanks to telecommunication and the Internet, it's possible to be in touch with one another, night and day. What most adults don't realize is that, to a teenager, these connections are not just a way to squander time, but rather a lifeline—a way of being heard and being known for who you believe you really are.

Finding a Comfort Zone

At the early levels of involvement, the second family is primarily a place of excitement, entertainment, and stimulation, reflecting all the values of the pop culture/peer group. But moving along the continuum, somewhere near the end of the *Exploration* level, the goal changes. The fun continues, but the *tyranny of cool* holds less power. Instead of trying to be in the A group, teenagers work toward the ultimate objective: *finding a comfort zone* (an aspiration of adults as well). At this juncture, the composition of the second family also changes. Gradually, stable subgroups begin to form around personalities, interests, and allegiances, much as in any system. Now the second family is a place of refuge that allows kids to shape a solid sense of identity. Eventually, teenagers find within it a niche into which they can comfortably slip, secure in the knowledge that there are others kids just like them.

Of course, teens have always tried to define themselves. But in this new scheme of adolescence, there are almost no peers telling them who or what they must be, few parents imposing values that a child must, in turn, overthrow. Young people are often left to their own devices, given a chance to try on different personas, even to reinvent themselves if necessary. As they strive to sort out who they are, they also seek to answer a second, more important question, "With whom do I feel most comfortable?"

Interestingly, peer hierarchy during much of the *Exploration* level is reminiscent of adolescence in old-think terms: inflexible and sometimes painful. A kid either has it or she doesn't; he's a nerd or a boy-boy. The *tyranny of cool* is at its height, and the values of the second family perfectly mirror the materialism of our culture. Much of the currency that goes toward popularity and leadership at this phase is what you'd expect—good looks, athletic prowess, and money, which, in turn, buys the latest gadgets and toys.

There's also a new coin of the realm among youngsters today—the art of dissing. In my talks to parents I refer to this as "everyday violence." It's often aimed at the unfortunately less-hip kids. And it hurts. But kids who possess this "skill" find themselves elevated in the pecking order. Even if a kid isn't physically attractive or doesn't dress well, if she's fast on her feet, adept at wisecracking and repartee, that's good enough for admission to the A group.

At this juncture, everyone's vying to be part of The Chosen. There's a great deal of comparison, and how well a child measures up can impact dramatically on his or her happiness. The barometers of popularity boil down to who's invited to the parties, who gives presents to whom, who calls whom after school, and who's on whose Internet "buddy list." It's all about status. Every kid wants to be king or queen and part of the most popular group. This is serious and often fierce competition—probably not unlike your own high school years.

The difference is, these kids are nine, ten, and eleven.

For the unpopular kids, though, relief comes at the *Comfort* level, usually in seventh or eighth grade, when peers splinter into subgroups and kids begin to find the courage to forge their own unique identities. This can be a great consolation to preteens like Luke or Sasha. Through sixth grade, they all but did backflips to get into the A group. Luke tried to dress like the popular kids, to be at their parties, but nothing worked because he lacked the ability to "diss" other kids. Sasha, an avid reader, tried to underplay her interest in books and to modify her own personality to be like whomever she happened to be with. She became what kids call "a floater"—not really part of any group.

Both Luke and Sasha started to change over the course of seventh and eighth grades. Discouraged and feeling uneasy in the struggle, Luke drifted toward kids around whom he at least felt comfortable. Like him, they weren't so verbally adept, not particularly trendy, and, if truth be told, a little bit on the nerdy side. Sasha eventually settled into a group of kids who looked more like holdover hippies than fashionable twelve-year-olds and who liked to read, were verbally articulate, and could discuss ideas.

Again, what we're seeing is that adolescence as we once understood it—a life stage during which a child first begins to sort out questions of identity—is changing. It not only happens at younger ages, it also reflects more of a desire for comfort than an attempt at rebellion. Both make sense. The culture at large values comfort; we are seeing our own desire reflected in our young people. Because of their easy intimacy with the pop culture, today's children are subjected to so much more adult content in the first ten years of their lives than kids in past generations. Whether this worldliness is good for them or not, the premature exposure apparently gives them an earlier sense of what they like and need—and, in turn, who they are. The second-family structure enables them to flow toward whatever feels easiest, to a place where they feel easy acceptance. After all, with other kids who are a bit klutzy, you don't have to explain why you're not on the baseball team. With other kids who love to read, you don't have to explain why you always have your nose in a book. Even supposed loners like Eric Harris and Dylan Klebold, the Columbine killers, found their niche in the second family. They had a circle of friends, kids similarly drawn to savage movies and videos, who took the boys' boasts in stride. Though Eric and Dylan ultimately distanced themselves with ever-increasing violence, their place in the second family was there for them until the very end.

A Conspiracy of Silence

Thankfully, few kids are as far gone as the Columbine killers. However, because teenagers have spent so much time in their separate universe and because they are so comfortable with "their kind," they are not merely reluctant to let us in, they erect an impenetrable wall of silence. This conspiracy, as it were, begins to tighten at the *Exploration* level and draws almost seamlessly closed at the *Comfort* level.

This was dramatically illustrated by a group of twelve- and thirteen-year-old girls at a sleep-away camp in the Southwest who spent eight weeks in the same bunk. These young women were not quite past the *Exploration* level, so what their friends thought and did was still enormously important. Kelly, one of the strongest personalities in the group, was slightly overweight and seriously obsessed with her appearance. She counted not only her own calories, but what the other girls ingested as well. When they sorted laundry, she read aloud the sizes of the other girls' clothing, offering a running commentary on who needed to lose weight and who didn't. By the fifth week of camp, a few of the other girls in the bunk, naturally susceptible to body-image problems themselves because of the cultural emphasis on thinness and beauty, were almost as obsessed with their weight as Kelly, and unwilling to participate in camp activities.

Of course, the girls didn't tell anyone about Kelly's problem, or how their own behavior had been affected. Neither the counselors nor the camp's two female directors were aware of what had been going on. One might assume—given old-think reasoning—that this conspiracy of silence was because no one wanted to "rat on" Kelly. But the truth was, these kids didn't want to risk adult involvement. They knew they'd be more carefully supervised, lose their freedom, and perhaps be forced to participate in required activities. In other words, every girl feared less the idea of being on her own than the prospect of inviting adult scrutiny.

Camp ended. The girls came home, and no adult was the wiser. The kids, who lived twenty-four/seven in the same bunk with three counselors, had managed to keep their worlds apart. Granted, teenagers have always been secretive. There has always been an unwritten code of loyalty: You don't rat on your friends; you don't tell adults about kid business. But teenage cover-ups today are motivated not just by honor or loyalty to one another. Like the girls in this bunk, most kids want the wide-open freedom of parallel worlds. The stakes are so much higher, and they simply don't want to do *anything* to invite adult scrutiny. When you're having that kind of unfettered access to peers and pop-culture fun and comfort, and are free to make your own decisions, talking to parents or teachers about what's really going on might just curtail your independence. Rather than run that risk, teens keep quiet. The only exception to this behavior is when a child is caught red-handed or when someone is literally in a life-or-death situation.

Fourteen-year-old Otto, for example, had stood by for several months watching his friend Stuart get into progressively more trouble with alcohol. Stuart could easily consume a six-pack of beer in a sitting; he regularly got drunk. Otto wrestled with his conscience. What if something really bad happened to Stuart? Still, he kept his concern to himself. One night, quite coincidentally because she happened to come down to the basement rec room when her son had several friends over, Otto's mother saw Stuart staggering around. Later, after the boys had gone, she talked to Otto, who finally admitted to her that he had been worried, too. Otto's mother saw Stuart's behavior as a cry for help, and she called his mother.

When Otto relayed the story to me, he was furious. "That's it. I'm never saying anything again," Otto lamented. "Stuart is grounded, and he won't talk to me. And word has gotten out that *I* got him busted."

Otto was right to be concerned. He *was* ostracized for almost a year. Quite different from what I'd learned to expect decades ago, there was no group or individual sigh of relief that Stuart received the help he needed. In fact, most of Otto's buddies didn't agree that Stuart was in real danger. One even commented, "Binge-drinking is no big deal." In his friends' view, Otto had interfered way before Stuart's situation had become a matter of life or death. Such circumstances were certainly not worth the subsequent adult intrusion.

Having heard similar scenarios from other kids, I am sure Otto will stick by his resolve. The wall of silence (now repeatedly documented by the investigators of schoolyard shootings), and the increased sophistication of our teens, are additional bits of evidence pointing to the power of the second family to subvert adult interference. Both the stakes and the tolerance for deviation are, indeed, higher.

The Surprisingly Hopeful News

So, you wonder, how could there be any *good* news? The second family, whether they label it as such or not, seems all too overwhelming to anyone who has to deal with today's kids. Certainly, stemming the tide of consumerism is out of our control. And though technology is moving faster than most of us would like, it has obvious benefits that we wouldn't want to eliminate.

But there is hopeful news: Although at face value it seems that the second family is an indestructible, if not malevolent force, in truth it isn't all bad. As many kids say to me, "I'm not who my parents [or teachers] think I am . . . I'm better." They're often right. As I explain in the next chapter, membership in the second family insulates teenagers from the harsher aspects of adolescence. They settle into a system that, to adults' wonderment, offers them support, understanding, and a set of values. As such, though filled with inherent dangers, this world apart may also bring out the best in our kids.

3

"I'm Not Who You Think I Am"
The Two Faces of Teens

The face teenagers show their parents is quite different from the face they show their friends. As if we're viewing the two-sided mask of Janus from one angle only, we adults don't get to see the other profile unless we somehow change our perspective. When we lay down our prejudices and see what is—rather than what we expect to see—we respect, even envy, teenagers. They can teach us not only how we need to treat them, but also what we're lacking in our own intimate relationships.

Today's Fear: Losing Kids to the Pop Culture

Parents have always pigeonholed other kids to some degree. Bert is the smart one—study with him. Fred's the star athlete—maybe you'll be included if you show up with him. Sara's the good kid—a positive influence. Or, they may find fault: George is stubborn; you're becoming just like him. Annie is fresh; stay away from her. But what I'm seeing lately is something new—beyond typecasting, beyond worrying about specific bad influences. *Parents fear aspects of the culture they see in their own kids.*

A father, appalled by his eight-year-old boy's incessant video-game-playing, says of his son, "He's so lazy. All he does is play with that damn Game Boy. No wonder he can't sit still in school." And I hear this from the mother of a nine-year-old girl in suburbia: "I can't even talk to Janie. She spends hours on-line, reading about the cast of *Popular*. And the language she uses. What if she turns out to be as self-centered as those kids on TV?"

Fear often runs through parents' conversations these days and underneath the timeworn worries is this new vein of apprehension: parents, even of elementary schoolers, are scared about their children's connection to the omnipresent second family. No matter how well-intentioned or effective they actually are, many mothers and fathers sense that their families are spinning out of control: in the battle over values, parents are dwarfed by the impact of the second family. It's not merely a matter of "losing children to the streets"—a misgiving many urban parents express. Now the threat is even bigger, an overwhelming danger that transcends the borders of the neighborhood, state, or even the country. Today's parents are afraid of losing their kids to the influences of pop culture and to that large, amorphous entity—their children's peer group.

I hear it in my office; I hear it in my workshops. I hear it from parents of all-aged children. In fact, a surprising number of adults, including principals and teachers, anticipate the worst from kids these days, particularly in the preteen and teen years: nastiness, disrespect, selfishness, lies, disconnection, conniving. Parents slip easily into this anxiety-driven put-down mode. Impelled by horrifying headlines and a sense of insignificance in the face of the high-tech explosion, they tend to develop a kind of tubular vision, which prevents them from seeing the bigger picture. They *think* they know their child, but they don't realize that they're describing only *parts* of him or her.

A health education teacher, a thirty-year veteran whom I met at an in-service workshop at a West Coast junior high, has observed an increasing schism over the last decade: "The teenager that parents see walking out the door is *not* the same kid we see in school. Part of my job is to get mothers and fathers and other adults who deal with teens to see beyond the obvious, past the more visible aspects, and to shift their view to the whole child."

The teacher is correct. Without actually using the term "second family," he was referring to the fact that children show a different face in the context of the peer culture. Seeing only one face both limits parents' understanding and confirms their vague fears. Ultimately, it makes them less effective because they're not truly "getting" who their child is.

Inside the Second Family

Many parents are astonished to learn that when they're with their buddies, children are very different from, often even the opposite of, the way they are at home or in the presence of other adults. Even more surprising, children's friends can bring out the best in them, especially during adolescence. It took me a long time as a therapist to accept this, even longer as a parent.

Hence, I say this with some trepidation: *The peer culture today, which is the bedrock of the second family, supports children in a way that too often we parents are failing to do.* When a preteen or teen settles into that secure niche in the *Comfort* level, he or she is given everything that "a family" is supposed to provide: sustenance, understanding, communication, ritual, and a host of values that kids can depend on. The second family has clear-cut expectations of its members and a structure that governs how kids act toward one another.

Within the second family, every child has what I call a *core group*, which kids often refer to as their "crew" or "posse." The core group is a kind of nuclear family, which comprises a teenager's closest, most intimate friends — kids who are like siblings. On the perimeter of a child's core group, there is also an extended family of friends — the *crowd*. This is the larger group, or clique, that your child pals around with. Talking to hundreds of kids, meeting their friends, and listening to their stories, I've come to see that if I want to know about a kid's interests, attitudes, and the general direction of his life, I look at the goings-on in his *crowd*. If I want to know about a child's feelings, I look at what's happening in his *core group*.

From the outside, a teen's crowd may have a unifying look that the kids all embrace. An outsider might identify the group as grunge, goody-goodies, hip-hop, retro hippies, dopers, airheads, preppies, jocks — or whatever label fits. The problem, as the health ed teacher described it, is that *those characteristics are often all that parents and other adults see.*

They look at the way the kids in a particular crowd dress, their mannerisms and interests, and then make judgments based on the outer trappings. But the inner dynamics—both what's going on inside a particular child and what her crowd believes in and stands for—are not quite so apparent.

For a long time, I missed that part of the picture, too. But listening carefully to the kids themselves taught me that how a given child interacts with the various and sundry adults in her life is often far different from—even diametrically opposed to—how she treats, and is regarded, by her friends. Once I became willing to look at and listen to these kids without bias, I was able to see that the second family is not only a black hole of danger but also offers kids a rich, connected world. To explain my own metamorphosis, I shall recount the stories of some of the kids who taught me that looking at how a child acts within his second-family crowd offers clues about what he or she needs from his first family. You may not find an exact description of your child in these stories, but look past the details. The overarching theme is that teenagers are often not who they seem to be.

Billy: The Amoral Slacker

Billy, a working-class boy of fourteen going on fifteen, very much like other kids I've met, had failed out of several schools, and was about to fail out of a third. His hair was dyed bright red with a blue streak in the front. He wore the characteristic baggy pants of a skateboarder and an earlobe full of silver rings. He played around with many girls, smoked pot erratically, but his parents, Marsha and Henry, were most concerned with the fact that no matter what they said or what his teachers insisted on, Billy simply didn't do his homework. He had barely graduated from elementary school, and his academics went downhill from there. Exasperated to the breaking point, Henry sometimes called him "lazy," "stupid," and "undependable." Marsha feared that Billy might be a lost cause.

Most of the adults in this boy's life felt the same way: here was an amoral kid—a teenager with no character. He spent half his time lying to and outwitting adults, running teachers ragged with excuses, and the rest of the time dodging them. The breaking point at school came after Billy had failed to show up for several appointments with a new math tutor. The math tutor had agreed to come in early on a Saturday morning. True to form, Billy was a no-show, ruining the man's weekend in the process. It appeared that Billy simply would never live up to his end of bargain.

No one in this boy's life, including me at first, even suspected that there was more to Billy than met the adult eye. At our initial session, although it was fairly obvious that he was smart, I said to myself, *What am I doing working with another kid like this?* But over the course of several months, as Billy described the ways in which he conducted himself with his friends, I began to see that he was everything to his peers that the adults in his world wished that he would be with them — loyal, caring, and dependable. One night, for instance, he stayed on the phone for seven hours with a girl whose beloved brother had died after a long bout with cancer. He vowed to take care of her. As he explained when he shared this story, "My word is my bond, and if she needs me, I'm there."

Imagine my confusion. This kid, who is supposedly "amoral," watches out for a friend, nurses her through a difficult emotional time. He is exactly what adults think he isn't. Despite his irresponsible behavior with the tutor, when he makes a plan to be somewhere with his friends, it's important to him that he sticks by it. Once he had asked several of his male friends to join him for a weekend picnic. They all committed to the date, but then Robbie, who had recently hooked up with a girl, told him he couldn't come. Billy was aghast.

"I'm a little disappointed," he explained, "but mostly I'm pissed because Robbie didn't keep his promise." He looked around my office for a second and tugged absently at the neck of his T-shirt. Then he turned and asked in all seriousness, "What matters more than his word?"

The most telling story about Billy concerned his growing attraction toward Becky. They had been good friends for years, part of each other's core group. As they began to get closer, Billy was delighted to feel their friendship going in a new direction but, at the same time, he anticipated another problem. Everyone knew that Ann, Becky's best friend, had a crush on Billy and might be jealous if he and Becky hooked up. Not wanting to create a problem in his "family," Billy addressed the situation head-on.

"If our relationship gets in the way of your friendship with Ann," he told Becky, "then you and I can't go out." Becky readily agreed; it was as if Billy had read her mind. She had already felt tormented by the thought that her developing relationship with Billy might make Ann feel left out. Still, the discussion about Ann deepened the bond between Billy and Becky. Despite their pact, the two spent increasing time with one another over the next several weeks. Finally, Billy suggested that they go to a movie—just the two of them.

Their worst fears were realized. Ann was jealous, consumed with rage, and embarrassed because everyone knew how she felt about Billy. Now she was "the loser." But here's the amazing part: Billy kept his word. "We can't go out anymore," he told Becky. "We're going to just have to be friends."

Don't get me wrong. Billy's no saint. He was furious with Ann for not being able to "get over herself." There were late-night phone calls and angry E-mails and a great deal of *Sturm und Drang* over the troubled triad, with assorted members of their crowd proffering commentary and advice. All the same, Billy made no further overtures to date Becky.

It was at that moment that I was able to really grasp how principled Billy was. What was happening in his relationships at home and with the adults at school had little to do with what I was seeing among his friends.

Eventually, by the way, Ann did settle down. She and Becky were able to talk through their difficulties and Ann was willing to forgive Becky, because their relationship meant a lot to her. Billy and Becky resumed dating.

I watched this all from the sidelines, astonished and, in a way, slightly envious that these kids were so fresh and alive, so connected to one another. Their relationships were richly textured, and their ability to be vulnerable with one another astounded me. *No wonder they're drawn to this world*, I said to myself, *so much goes on within it*. Ultimately, my empathy provided a key to connect with Billy and to help his parents understand what they needed to do to get through to him. It also opened my eyes to similar dualities in other kids.

Alicia: The Bitch

At home, Alicia seemed nasty to the core. Superficially an all-American suburban girl, she not only had a quick comeback and an answer for everything, she always had to be right. She was verbally adept, a natural-born mimic, but unfortunately she used these talents to cut everyone down. She was, in her own mother's words, "a real bitch." Alicia had an uncanny gift for zeroing in on people's foibles. She'd berate her mother for "going on and on about things" or for getting hysterical over the slightest problem. She'd accuse her father of acting pompous. And she often picked on her nine-year-old brother Evan, calling him "a fat tub of lard," among other invectives.

The worst aspect of Alicia's biting sarcasm was that her barbs were always based on some degree of reality. She sensed people's vulnerabilities and, at the least provocation or when she didn't get what she wanted, she went right for the jugular. She knew that her mother didn't always feel in control of emotions, that her father worried because he didn't feel as smart as people thought he was, and that Evan felt slightly chubby. She didn't seem to care that her verbal torrents made them feel worse.

Alicia's deteriorating relationships with her family earned her a weekly appointment at my office. The twelve-year-old I met was smart, pretty, and involved in school — clearly, part of the popular crowd. Put to good use, of course, her radar and her ability to see people so incisively was a gift, but Alicia's parents couldn't imagine their daughter in any other context than the family. They only saw the Alicia who lived in a bedroom on the second floor. But I got to hear what went on when this young woman was away from home.

The more I listened to Alicia, the more I realized that this so-called bitch was also a caretaker. Although she was quick and sometimes acerbic with her friends, too, within her core group such "dissing" was appreciated, even admired, so no one thought badly of her. Perhaps that was because her friends knew what her family didn't: there was more to

Alicia than her sharp tongue. She was always worried about this friend or that. Among her peers, she was known for being fair-minded and solution-oriented. In fact, one anecdote after another highlighted Alicia's gift for getting other kids through difficult situations.

When her friend Tina talked about her father, an insulting, sometimes physically brutal man, Alicia listened thoughtfully and compassionately. After a long talk she convinced Tina to call an abuse hot line.

When Matt was concerned because his parents were heavily into pot, Alicia offered to have him hang out at her house after school instead. Ironically, it was one of the few times Alicia was civil to her mother, because she wanted to help Matt "connect" with a good parent!

When her close friend Maya started obsessing over food and vomiting in the bathroom, Alicia organized several other girls in her core group to help. Four of them went to a trusted guidance counselor and, so as not to divulge specific information about Maya, asked, "What could we do if we suspected that one of our friends had an eating disorder?"

And when Darcy, a fellow seventh-grader who was part of the crowd, told Alicia she had access to a veritable pharmacy of illicit drugs—including acid, 'shrooms, and Ecstasy—she tried to steer Darcy, who apparently had an older brother trafficking at the high school, in a less-destructive direction.

"I told her that I wasn't interested in taking any of those things. But I also told her that it wasn't too smart to be selling drugs," Alicia explained. "She could get caught so easily."

Again, there was contradiction: Alicia was cruel at home but kind to her peers. She was seemingly uncaring with her family but deeply sensitive to her friends' needs. She had more than her share of common sense and insight but that side of her was under wraps at home, reserved only for the late-night consultations with members of her other family. My job was to acquaint her parents with the hidden parts of Alicia, and to help her trust them enough to show all of herself to them.

Tony: The Disconnected Kid

In a case I supervised long-distance, over the phone, the counselor described the "two faces of teens" phenomenon. His client was an adolescent named Tony. Tony's parents, Marsha and John, often couched their true feelings about him by saying to friends that their son, a talented fine artist, was "sensitive" and often "in his own world." Privately, they admitted Tony was disconnected, hard to decipher, and frequently downright cold toward them. Tony is gay and had recently come out, a fact that they didn't take too seriously, because he was only fourteen. But, they assured the therapist, "If that's what he chooses, it's okay with us. We just wish he'd act a little bit more like he's part of this family."

Tony was doing well in school and was part of a tightly knit core group. His crowd, not surprisingly, was considered "the arty crowd." His best friend was Maggie, whom he called every night for at least an hour, if not longer. Often, the two fell asleep with receivers still cradled to their ears.

Although Tony thought of Maggie as his best friend, she would have liked to be more than friends. Their relationship was obviously not destined to go in that direction. And the more Tony got in touch with his sexuality, the more Maggie had to be satisfied with what they had — a rich, nourishing friendship. And, for the most part, she was . . . until Tony began to talk about Sean, a boy he liked. As the boys' relationship developed, Maggie finally had to accept that Tony would never feel about her the way he did about Sean. This did not happen, though, without a mad frenzy of E-mail and phone calls among various members of Maggie and Tony's crowd, everyone getting into the act, taking sides, trying to make peace.

One of the amazing aspects of Tony's story, not unusual for gay or straight kids, is that almost none of these goings-on were apparent to his parents. Marsha and John knew their son spent time on the phone talking to Maggie and to other friends, but they remained steadfast in their view of Tony as "too disconnected." They had few clues that their boy was surrounded by such a supportive network of kids, or that he devoted so much time discussing what mattered to him, connecting on a deep, emotional level. They didn't realize that he often acted the mediator when other kids got into a dispute. Or that while he was busy chatting with four or five kids on-line, he would be on the phone as well, helping someone else with math homework. It was the same with his camp friends. Just about every night, there was some communication, often a drama unfolding, and Tony was in the thick of it—who likes whom, who said what about whom, who's going to be at this party or that.

Again, this case reinforced the fact that for all the negatives we ascribe to the second family, its structure also supports intimacy, communication, and honesty among kids. Through the descriptions of his counselor, I watched Tony negotiate delicate feelings and reach inside himself for compassion and understanding. Most important, I saw that Tony's life in the second family was exactly opposite of what he let his parents and other adults see. And the more Tony's parents thought of him as uncaring, arrogant, and disconnected, the more hurt and the less open they were to understanding what was really going on.

Ursula: Hopelessly Rebellious

Ursula, at fifteen, seemed to want nothing to do with her stay-at-home mother or her father, a high-powered computer salesman. Clearly, their painful situation at home was fraught with troubles beyond their control. Within a two-year period, Ursula's aunt had died, and her eighteen-year-old brother, who had run away several times, had become a hard-core substance abuser.

Ursula's father, in particular, was beside himself, remembering his own rebellious youth. Ursula talked back constantly and regularly defied the few rules her parents set. She often stayed out way past her curfew, hanging out with large groups of girls and boys. Dad was sure that at this point, his daughter, who was quite pretty and physically mature for her age, was sleeping around and, ultimately, headed for even more serious danger.

"Is Ursula destined to go her brother's route?" he wondered aloud when we met, "or is she just another hopelessly rebellious adolescent?"

Sadly, neither Mom or Dad had never seen the side of Ursula I was then privileged to witness. Nor did they know what really went on in Ursula's crowd. Ursula had nestled herself into a secure network of support, composed of both kids from school and those she knew from camp. Several boys were part of her core group, but they were her friends, not her sex partners. Ursula's friends not only knew about her inner turmoil, her grief, and the private guilt she suffered, they also tried to help her deal with it all. For example, she blamed herself for what had gone wrong in her family. When her brother ran away, she "should have seen the signs." When her beloved aunt died, she had been involved in some serious arguments with her, so they parted on uneasy terms.

Once she knew I respected her friendships, the allegedly truculent Ursula loved to talk to me about her crew: Brian, who patiently tried to relieve her of her guilt; Sarah who got mad when Ursula drank too much; Debbie, who told her to "give your mother a break." I was astounded to hear Ursula talk this way and to realize how different she was from the way her parents portrayed her, especially because her mother was utterly convinced that Ursula's friends were a "bad influence." Mom was sure that to help her daughter, she had to keep her away from those kids. "I'll never understand them," she told me, "and they'll never understand me." More despairing than even Dad, Mom not only wrote off Ursula's friends, she was giving up on her own daughter, too. Like many parents she concluded, "There's no sense in my expecting her to talk to me. Kids never talk to their parents, I didn't talk to mine. I just have to be careful to limit her access to these kids."

Both Ursula's mother and father failed to recognize that peer support was central in their daughter's life—in fact, the healthiest part of her existence. The phone calls, the conversations, the love and caring they provided helped Ursula cope with the adversities within her family and also helped her to heal. But as long as Mom and Dad maintained an us-versus-them stance, they would continue to see their daughter in one-dimensional terms.

Frank: The Liar

Frank was sent to me because he was failing in school, and nothing anyone said or did seemed to get through to him. Like many of the teens I meet, he lied to his parents, to his teachers, to me. At the outset of our sessions, he missed one appointment after another, always with a "good reason." Here was a boy who elevated "the cat ate my homework" to new heights.

Frank was fourteen when we met, tall and physically mature for his age. Over the course of the next year, when I began to listen carefully to sagas about Frank and his friends, here, too, I saw a young man who had a far different side to him—qualities that the adults in his life never got to see. Where we all thought he couldn't tell a story without lying, his friends respected his honesty and his ability to express exactly how he felt.

The incident that crystallized this disparity centered on Frank's relationship with Jeff, a name that cropped up repeatedly in our sessions. Although Frank admired Jeff, he was also very jealous of his best friend—a classically good-looking guy who, in Frank's words, "could get any girl he wanted." With Frank's striking hazel eyes and jet-black hair, he was extremely attractive himself, wore clothes well, and had a winning smile. Still, Frank didn't *feel* handsome—an insecurity betrayed only by his unconscious habit of chewing on the left side of his lower lip. And, in truth, girls didn't pursue him the way they went after Jeff, who exuded confidence.

Finally, just as Frank was about to turn fifteen, his luck with girls seemed to change. Rachel let it be known she had a crush on him. He looked for her in school, spent time with her on the phone at night, and sent her endless E-mail. Soon, they were together. Frank wasn't doing any better in school, mind you, but he did seem more at ease with himself.

One day, Frank told me that he was really angry because at a party over the weekend Rachel and Jeff had kidded around with each other a little too much. "They were definitely flirting. I thought he was moving in on me."

Uh, oh, I said to myself, *this could end badly*. Imagining a similar scenario from my own boyhood, I was sure Frank would either fight with Jeff or end the friendship, refusing to even talk about it. But that's not what happened. To my surprise, Frank asked Jeff to come over to his house. When Jeff got there, Frank took a few beers from the refrigerator (he was fourteen, but still wanted to be a good "host") and led Jeff to the garage, a place they often hung out and talked.

Frank pulled no punches. He said to Jeff, "I can't stand it when you get so chummy with Rachel. At that party, it looked like you could have hooked up with her if you wanted. I know it's not cool, but I get jealous of you."

Jeff listened. He didn't put Frank down or tell him he was wrong for feeling that way. Frank continued: "I know I'm crazy. I shouldn't be this uptight. But I am. So I'm asking you, please . . . don't put your arm around Rachel. And try not to be so smooth with her."

As Frank related this conversation, I thought to myself, *this is impossible*. I couldn't believe that this boy, or any boy, would say those things to a friend. I didn't think he had the language to express his feelings, let alone the courage to share them with another boy. The young men I met ten or fifteen years ago and certainly the boys of my own youth couldn't have conversations with one another unless they were about sports, girls, or cars—certainly not about *feelings*. Sure, many boys still lack what Michael Nerney, a nationally respected school consultant, calls, "emotional literacy." Yet change is in the air. My old-think expectation, based on increasingly outdated ideas about boys, was that Frank would lash out at Jeff in some way. Or, he might turn his rage against himself and get into even more trouble at school or with his parents. Instead, this boy whom we all thought of as a liar astounded me with his honesty. This boy whom no adult could reach was able to be intimate and vulnerable with his best friend.

Second-Family Standards

Frank and other kids helped me realize that what we adults see in our homes, our classrooms, and our offices, is quite different from and, often, the opposite of, how teenagers behave in the second family. The same youngsters who are estranged from their parents care deeply about and feel connected to their peers. They are reluctant to open up to adults but can communicate with one another. And though they may often refuse to take part in their first family, they create an array of meaningful rituals that keep them glued to the members of their second family.

In other words, these kids live in an alternate reality. The "amoral" Billy is rigorously devoted to his friends. "Nasty" Alicia can be kind and helpful. "Disconnected" Tony is exquisitely sensitive. "Rebellious" Ursula appreciates the give-and-take within her cocoon of support. And Frank, "the liar," is a stand-up guy, whom peers can depend on.

What's going on? Perhaps it is difficult to believe, but the second family can bring out the best in kids. It gives them what they often don't get from busy parents or teachers, who are preoccupied and stretched to their limits—a sense of comfort, belonging, rules, rituals, and honest feedback. When I began to understand this and to respect the standards teenagers applied toward themselves and one another, I was finally able to see the individuals and their peer network in a way that I was never formally taught as a practitioner to do (or, for that matter, as a parent, looking at my own children). I could see that both within the core group and the larger crowd, they found the comfort that goes with acceptance and very clear rules of conduct.

We ought to learn from the peer culture. Granted, there are still feuds within it, still kids that are abandoned to the fringes, still too much competitiveness, and way too much cruelty among children. The second family can be extremely dangerous and hazardous to a child's health. But seeing *only* that side is inaccurate and won't make the problem go away. At the same time, particularly within a kid's core group, communication, respect, and a willingness to express feelings are not only commonplace, they are expected. Rituals are embraced for their constancy and their meaning. Along with the live-and-let-live ethos, there's a do-unto-others attitude that governs the way kids act. As a result, *we are seeing a new generation of teens who are more honest, open, and willing to put their feelings on the line with their friends than adolescents once were.*

Remember that children and adults have been relegated to separate worlds in our culture and children grow up living parallel to their elders. As thirteen-year-old Winston recently remarked, "We're not arguing with our parents like you did. We're off on our own, we're not even noticing them that much." By the time kids like Winston reach early adolescence they're used to flying solo, without the scrutiny or interference of adults.

As I will point out below, kids are exploring new territory; a lot of teen-ager's basic needs—to connect, to have fun, to belong, to communicate and, most of all, to find comfort—are satisfied by evolving (and often secret) relationships with their peers.

Gender Bending

Perhaps most astonishing is that the new standards apply equally to boys *and* girls. Yes, one "boy book" after another, among them Daniel Kind-lon's and Michael Thompson's brilliant *Raising Cain* and William Pol-lack's soulful *Real Boys*, tells us that young males, unable to voice their feelings, give vent to them physically instead—through positive outlets, such as in sports, or maladaptive means, such as general unruliness or sadism. Likewise, a spate of books about girls, such as Carol Gilligan's prescient *In a Different Voice* and Mary Pipher's startling *Reviving Ophe-lia*, vividly demonstrate the notion that girls' confidence is compromised by the culture, that they're unequal participants on the playing fields of sex and gamesmanship, and that we need to help them become more assertive and proactive. To be sure, those authors have made enormous contributions to our understanding of gender socialization. They define pervasive problems in our culture and are on target.

However, because looking at either gender *separately* creates a slightly different perspective, the changing male/female relationships within the second family are not always illustrated. Of course, *many* boys' trou-bles—drinking, carousing, vandalizing—can be attributed to pent-up male aggression or identification with extreme male stereotyping; *many* girls are more shy and self-effacing in public than they really are. I grant that you will find typecast males and females at either end of the gender continuum, but because the cultural environment is changing so rap-idly, kids in the middle don't always fit the mold, and we can no longer hold pre-Millennium views of boys and girls as universal truths.

More than we realize, kids *are learning* to talk to one another. Be-cause of what they've absorbed from the pop culture, not to mention the emphasis on communication skills in most schools (in no small measure, because of the impact the aforementioned authors, among many others), teenagers are beginning to learn how to speak the language of feelings. One of the first pop-culture markers of this sea of change actually dates back to 1985 when John Hughes's *The Breakfast Club* was released. Still a favorite of kids today, the movie featured a group of mismatched teenagers—a jock, a rich bitch, a metalhead, a weirdo, and a nerd—thrown together in Saturday morning detention. The unlikely group, forced together by their collective fate, opened up to one another, discussed feelings, bared secrets. In effect, they took part in an encounter group—ironically, a therapeutic form that their parents' generation first embraced. Fifteen years later, we're seeing the trickle-down effect. At least one program a night, whether it's *Dawson's Creek, Popular, Freaks and Geeks, Caitlin's Way,* or *Seventh Heaven*, depicts kids working out complex relationship issues in their everyday lives. And because producers are aware that kids comprise a large part of the day-time TV audience, soap operas now feature more teen-targeted story lines, as do talk shows, many of which air during after-school hours. In fact, by the nature of the topics on talk shows ("I was a teenage hooker," "My mom hates the way I dress"), one can't help believing that producers have teens in mind.

Night and day, then, TV characters talk about problems with parents, date rape, unrequited love, sexual firsts, anger, betrayal, depression—you name it. All of these discussions are now part of their everyday life, and kids carry the lessons and the skills into their own personal and private dramas. Girls are still more expressive than boys, but the gap has narrowed considerably. Emotions and confidences are shared across gender lines.

Consider Tamika, a thirteen-year-old girl I counseled. She was tormented over her parents' divorce and the fact that her older sister had recently gotten married, leaving Tamika on her own to deal with the massive changes in her family life. Her coping strategy was to break into her parents' liquor cabinet. In past sessions, Tamika, whom I'd known for a year, was typically antagonistic and rebellious, but, with her sister's departure, she became alarmingly despondent. Suspecting that she might be suicidal, I asked, "Who in your group of friends would you turn to if something really bothered you? Who would you really trust if you needed help?"

To my surprise, she answered, "Tommy and Kirk. They're my closest friends. Laurie and Wendy are good friends, too, but I can really talk to Tommy and Kirk." It's no mere coincidence that a week later, finally breaking the teenage wall of silence, Tommy and Kirk called Tamika's mother and said they were worried about her—she seemed so "down." The boys—observing the second-family code of not including adults unless it's a life-and-death situation—told Tamika's mother point blank, "Mrs. Washington, we're scared Tamika might do something bad to herself."

Interestingly, the narrowing gender gap has also changed the make-up of my teenage client population. Once all boys, it's now fifty-fifty. Ten or fifteen years ago, teenage girls avoided male therapists. I'd never have seen a Tamika, an Alicia, or an Ursula in my office, because they simply wouldn't open up to a man or feel comfortable talking about personal matters. Today, girls have far less difficulty talking about their periods, sex, or birth control in my presence—it's everyday parlance in their world. If they can talk to boys about these things, why not to me?

Communication and the Gift of Emotional Entitlement

Teenagers of both genders also believe they *deserve* to be listened to. In part, this is the result of a decade of child-centered parenting, in which many parents have gone overboard to make sure their kids feel "heard." Understandably, children now expect to be listened to and expect that what they say will be taken seriously. So, when a kid like Frank decides to have a heart-to-heart talk with his buddy, Jeff, only for a brief moment did he worry that Jeff might not listen or might put him down. Frank knew that Jeff would be willing to talk; he knew that what he had to say to his best friend probably would be taken seriously. Like many kids nowadays, he feels entitled to have his emotional day in court.

The Internet has also furthered the cause of communication among kids. Being on-line allows kids to say things to each other that they might not say face-to-face. Of course, there's a negative side to chat-room and Instant Message talk—bad language, put-downs, even life threats. But we can't ignore the fact that this new media is a training ground where kids, like Maggie and Tony, learn how to take care of interpersonal business. As Billy once confessed to me, "I like talking on-line, because I don't have to see the other person's face if I've made them feel bad." This is obviously good and bad. The negative is often cited, but the other side—the fact that these chats can improve a child's communication skills—is ignored by many social commentators.

Clearly, past generations could never have imagined the avenues of communication open to modern teens. More than variety, though, phone and fax and E-mail are the tools kids use to work problems out, to give each other constant feedback, and, most important, to stay in touch.

Rituals of Connection

The second family offers endless rituals of connection and belonging. Kids always check in with members of their core group, whether it's by electronic means or by finding time during the school day to say hello and catch up. I've heard from many teenagers, not just Maggie and Tony, that they call each other before bedtime and often fall asleep with receivers in their ears. Many modern kids go on-line every night to share with one another the vagaries of their day. Some watch favorite weekly TV shows together, while hanging out on the phone. And, in almost every case, these rituals usually begin before adolescence.

Boys and girls often meet after school or at least have weekly standing dates. One group I knew met every Friday to see a movie, and they did this from the time they were in seventh grade until they went off to college. Another group, whose parents dragged them off to church every Sunday, made the best of a "boring" demand by making sure that when their families went out to lunch following services, they sat at a separate table. A bevy of suburban eighth-graders I knew considered Saturday their "mall day" (along with countless millions of others).

Teenagers also create rituals of initiation—admittedly, sometimes around adult-disapproved activities, like drinking or piercing. Fourteen-year-old Jenny told me that she and her gang were getting together this weekend, "because it's going to be the first time Karen takes a drink." Within every second-family subgroup, everyone knows who has done what, when it's someone's first time, when kids are scared and when they're ready. There's no pressure to conform, but there certainly is support.

Daniel, a twelve-year-old boy whose parents had absolutely forbidden him to have his ear pierced, had no trouble getting his friends to help him find a "good, clean place" to have it done and to go with him. I hear this all the time, whether it's about weird haircuts, tattooing, or piercing—it's usually done with other kids. Only in rare and blessed circumstances is any parent involved. Think about it: how many mothers or fathers do you know who would willingly take part in such events? Sadly, most parents have trouble suspending judgment about their kids' appearance, interests, and activities.

Turning Envy into Insight

When adults can bring themselves to abandon the old prejudices about kids and their peers, they are often awed, as I have been, by the succor and wisdom that teenagers give one another. But we have to be willing to really look at who they are and at what's going on in their lives. The mountain won't come to Mohammad; we must travel to their world. And, as painful as this may be to accept, given the standards, the support, and the sacred rituals of the second family, in the context of the frenetic, fractured pace of first-family life, *teenagers today have little reason to attach themselves to their parents or other adults.* Most of their needs—to connect, to belong, and to communicate—are satisfied by members of their second family.

In one family I can recall, the parents had decided to get divorced because the father, who was secretly gay, had finally come out. The adults agonized for months before breaking it to Bart, then sixteen. As it turned out, their son had suspected the truth about his father's sexuality and had already worked through many of his feelings by talking to his friends, who listened and gave him their unconditional support. Even as things were crumbling at home, Bart's second family was holding him up. Once his parents were more straightforward, they could effect at least a similar gravitational pull on their son and, together, set about changing the family form in a less-disruptive and painful way. As Bart's mother put it, "Things have changed so much. The sexual part of our breakup, which was what we were so concerned about, was no big deal—partly, I realize, because his friends had helped him through it."

When they peek into the private world of the second family, parents sometimes envy their children. They realize that their kids are bolstered by their relationships with friends. In fact, many of today's teenagers seem to be doing just about everything that advice books suggest to adults who want to deepen their intimacy. They make time for one another. On a daily basis, and from morning until night, they build and maintain their relationships. Rather than stockpile their feelings, they make attempts to say what's on their minds. They create rituals of initiation and belonging. Granted, they are just teenagers, so they don't have the benefit of years or the ability to look back and correct their course as an adult does. Still, these kids often exemplify what they need from us and, not so incidentally, what we're lacking in our own relationships.

As I said at the outset of this chapter, teenagers present us with a two-sided mask. If we look at our children from one angle only, we don't get to see the other profile. Because kids have taught me to think about their networks of friends in a new way, I have been able to see both sides of my young clients' faces. This work has shown me that somehow I have to teach other adults who deal with teens—not only parents, but teachers, principals, coaches, and clergy—how to change their perspective so that they, too, might begin to see the other side.

To do this, we must travel to our kids' world. In the next chapter, I explain how I help adults understand and gain respect for a child's other profile and for the alien terrain of Planet Youth—a place most are reluctant to travel to. I get them to observe the teenager they don't know. In the end, I hope to encourage adults to provide a balance, which consists of the understanding, support, and sustenance their teenagers get from the second family, as well as the guidance that only compassionate, experienced, and knowledgeable grownups can provide.

4

"Why Don't You Invite Your Friends Over?"

Dealing with the Second Family

Successful parents and other adults who connect with teens embrace, rather than reject, the second family. They also strike a balance between empathy and expectations. Instead of trying to create "quality time" with kids, they share "comfort time." These adults talk to teens and their friends about issues they'd never have dreamed of discussing with their own parents—and, in the process, discover that Planet Youth is both more forbidding and yet more accessible than they assumed it would be.

Life Imitates Art

Watching reruns of the first season of *The Sopranos,* I was struck by one scene in particular, because it crystallized the gap between parents and their teenagers. For those of you who are unfamiliar with the HBO series, its centers on the life and times of one Anthony (Tony) Soprano, a "wise guy" in northern New Jersey. In this particular scene, which takes place at breakfast, Tony joins his wife, Carmella, and their two children, Meadow, fifteen, and her younger brother, Anthony Jr., who is around twelve. Carmella is at the stove, using a spatula to jiggle eggs in a frying pan. Tony, in his bathrobe, sips orange juice while watching the morning news on television. The kids chow down at the counter.

From the TV, a disembodied voice informs us that a policeman was apprehended in a bordello raid, along with several figures from the underworld. At the end of the report, the male TV anchor remarks to his female co-host, "I don't know which is more embarrassing—to be caught in a bordello or to be caught with a wise guy."

Disgusted, Tony turns off the television, at which point, Anthony Jr. asks, "What's a bordello?"

Without skipping a beat, Meadow matter-of-factly answers, "It's a fancy name for a whorehouse."

Carmella shoots her a dirty look. "Don't start, okay?"

Meadow (innocently): "It *is*."

"Yeah, I know it is," says Carmella, "but I just don't like that talk."

Meadow, indignant, continues, as if she's reciting from a report she's prepared for school: "This country is light-years behind the rest of the world. Most civilized countries have legalized prostitution . . ."

"Don't you got somewhere to be?" Tony interrupts his daughter in a tough Mafioso manner.

Meadow, unfazed, *goes on*. "I mean it's a joke. Look at what they're putting the president through." (This was the 1999 season.)

Carmella jumps in: "He got what he deserved."

"He *got* Monica Kozinsky [sic]," Anthony Jr. corrects, "and the broad with the long nose."

Meadow, still on her soapbox, clarifies her position: "I just don't think sex should be a punishable offense."

Tony is clearly getting exasperated, but his response is controlled. "You know, honey, that's where I agree with you. I don't think sex should be a punishable offense either. But I do think that talking about sex at the breakfast table *is* a punishable offense. So no more sex talk, okay?"

Meadow calmly replies, "It's the nineties. Parents are supposed to discuss sex with their children."

"Yeah, but that's where you're wrong," Tony says, looking out the window. "You see, out there, it's the nineties. In here, it's 1954." Visibly annoyed, he finally ends the discussion: "So now and forever, I don't want to hear any more sex talk, okay?"

There's Never Been a Better Time to Talk

In households across America, similar scenes are being played out. Other (real) mothers and fathers might not be quite so direct as Tony, but their actions amount to the same message: *Don't talk, don't tell.* Commercials sponsored by Drug-Free America, as well as other public-service announcements, acknowledge this conundrum. Kids *need* their parents to talk to them about drugs, but sometimes it's we parents, not the kids, who are reticent. Of course, many kids put up a huge wall, but more often, teenagers are both willing and able to talk about sex, substances, and other subjects that, until now, would never have come up at the breakfast table or in any other context, for that matter.

This is hard for most parents to accept. After all . . .

Could you imagine talking to your parents about kids "hooking up" at a party? About blow jobs, group sex, genital-piercing?

Could you imagine telling your parents that other kids pick on you because you're fat? Or that you're a "loser"?

Could you imagine discussing with your parents the fact that boys get drunk to have the courage to approach girls?

Could you imagine talking to your parents about kids abusing pot, Ritalin, 'shrooms, Ecstasy?

Could you imagine talking to your parents about eating disorders?

Could you imagine voicing concerns about your sexuality or coming out to your parents as bi or gay?

If you've answered "no" to all of these questions, you're obviously not a modern adolescent. Thirty years ago, teenagers lacked the vocabulary, the openness, and, perhaps most important, the blessing of the culture at large to consider even bringing up such subjects with their parents. That's why too many mothers and fathers today can't imagine that *their* kids would ever be willing to talk to them.

They're wrong. In fact, these are precisely the kinds of conversations teenagers are having with one another. And, as much as they may re-flexively run away or change the subject when we initially broach these topics, most kids are not completely against talking to us about once-taboo matters as well. Some, like the fictitious Meadow, actually do make impassioned speeches to their parents. They think their parents *owe* them these discussions! After all, they've seen numerous TV parents and kids having them.

There are several reasons why there has never been a better time than this to talk to kids about what really matters. The societal upheaval of the '60s, which compelled Dylan to sing, "The times they are a-changin'," has reached critical mass, ushering in a new paradigm:

We have brought out into the open what was once only whispered behind closed doors. Consider, if you will, that even in the last few decades, aside from oral sex in the Oval Office, an unprecedented number of dramatic private happenings have gone public: O. J. standing trial for murder and, in the process, baring a history of domestic violence; Callista Flockhart, aka "Ally McBeal," defending herself against allegations of anorexia; tabloids spreading suspicion about Leonardo diCaprio's sexual orientation; Anita Hill accusing Clarence Thomas of sexual harassment. As a result of these and a host of other headlines, once-unspeakable topics have become dinner-table conversation. Some of what was once aberrant (and abhorrent) behavior is now merely different in most people's eyes. In short, our children have grown up in a world of wide-open parameters. Through television, movies, and their own peer network, they have been exposed to everything and anything—sex and serial murders, abuse and alcoholism, drugs and a dizzying range of psychological disorders. For better or worse, there are few topics kids haven't already heard.

Since the late '70s in the culture at large, we've also seen the rise of the "caring and sharing" movement, as pollster George Gallup characterizes the growth of quasi-therapeutic groups. Strangers now bare their souls in public forums ranging from protests to TV talk shows to twelve-step programs. As a result, the language of therapy is part and parcel of our everyday speech; as such, it is also part of our kids' vernacular. Hence, because teens have the vocabulary as well as some rudimentary understanding, they are capable of discussions we never would have dreamed of having with our folks. They are neither humiliated by nor shy about handling subjects that would have mortified us as kids.

We are swimming in the same cultural seas as our kids. Despite the gulf between adults and children, both generations absorb the same messages, even buy the same products. This became quite clear in the late '80s, with the simultaneous publication of Madonna's music video and her book entitled *Sex*. As parents brought home the book in brown paper bags and hid it away in their closets, or sneaked peeks at a friend's copy, their kids were not only watching the video on MTV, they were fully aware of the publishing event that their parents were trying to suppress. (I dare say, many kids probably also ferreted out their parents' not-so-secret copy of the book as well.)

In more recent years, this blurring of age boundaries has escalated. In a recent *New York Times* article (August, 2000) the headline read, "Once the defining line of the generation gap, music taste is now shared by parents and children." The *Times* article highlights rock concerts. In addition, other national phenomena, such as wrestling, talk shows, and chat rooms, transcend generational boundaries. Every day kids and adults watch the same talk shows (perhaps on different TV sets) with titles, language, and visuals that range from the clearly obscene to the frankly dangerous. Adults and children often visit the same Web sites, for information or titillation. Many kids tell me about conversations with strange adults of all ages in Internet chat rooms. Whether the subject is cars or sex, the stock market or celebrity gossip, few care how old anyone is, just as long as he or she is willing to talk.

There's little generational warfare. Teenagers don't mind the world we've created. In fact, they want to be part of it. *They want in on adult matters.* Yes, kids still argue with their parents, label their rules "unfair," are wildly disrespectful toward their elders. But they're not at war; they have no desire to overthrow the hated adult establishment, as we once did.

Many teenagers, in fact, are willingly involved with adults — just not the ones in the first family at home. One fifteen-year-old boy I know told me that grownups twice his age go on-line and play video games, too. He has developed a significant relationship with a forty-year-old woman, his cyber "mother" in a fantasy game on the Web, which he's been playing for two years. Tens of thousands of adults and kids are into other fantasy games. Likewise, there are many Web sites for celebrities, songs, groups, movies, and TV programs that bring together cyberparticipants from several generations.

This combination of factors—that kids have the exposure, the familiarity, and the vocabulary and, at the same time, lack that unrelenting animosity toward adults seen in previous generations—means that the door is open. Teenagers often don't show it, but they want us to walk in.

Sadly, we don't always respond to the invitation.

Frightened and Stuck in Old-Think Heads

In part, the problem is that we assume our kids are the way we were. We didn't want to talk to our parents, so why would our kids want to talk to us? I remember when I was a kid, if I were watching a movie on TV with my mother and father, and the characters started kissing, I'd want to shrink from view. I was embarrassed to be in the same room with my parents, much less risk that either of them might acknowledge what was happening on screen. Of course, no one ever said anything. Likewise, when my friends came into the house, I dreaded my parents saying more than "hello." God forbid they should start a real conversation! Most parents have similar memories, and they assume that these rules are essentially still true for kids today.

"Teenagers only want to hang out with each other," Joanna's mother insisted, when I first suggested that to deal with her daughter's bitchiness, she try to both talk to her daughter about what's happening in her life and even talk to her friends. "They don't want any part of me. And if I try, I'm sure Joanna is going to get nastier than ever."

Her reaction is not uncommon. But the problem runs even deeper than parents' own pasts or their pessimism. Many adults are repulsed by the adolescent world—and, more significant, feel that the goings-on are simply not for their eyes. They find the music repugnant, the media distasteful. They use words like "stupid," "raw," "in-your-face," and "a waste of time" to describe teenagers' taste and activities. Now that may not sound new—at first, most grownups thought Elvis Presley was vulgar. But the scope was different in earlier times; the media didn't loom so large and wasn't so invasive; it didn't reach every house or beam into our living rooms twenty-four/seven. As a result, there was more of a balance between the kids' world and the various institutions that represented family, neighborhood, and the religious community.

Equally important, our parents' distaste reflected true generational warfare. They worried about our morality; today, that's a nonissue. As many current surveys of social beliefs demonstrate, people do worry about the permissiveness of our culture, but they are even more concerned about reverting to a strict authoritarian society, which our parents' generation thought was the "answer" to our own teenage rebellion. What alarms adults more than either permissiveness or rigidity is violence. Given the headlines and horrific events that involve teenagers, parents fear that every child, perhaps their own or someone else's, is a time bomb. As a mother recently said to me, "I'm less interested in absolute right and wrong . . . I just want to know that my kid is going to be *alive*."

In the face of such fears, parents often feel overwhelmed. When I suggest that they take an interest in the pop-culture offerings that attract their children, many are like Joanna's mom. They say to me, "What's the use? What good will it do for me to talk to them about these things?" Mothers and fathers realize they *should* find out where their kids go, what they talk about, and what they're dealing with on a day-to-day basis, but the prospect is daunting. As one mother in a workshop admitted in front of several hundred other parents, "I'd rather not know. It's easier. As soon as I know, I feel I have to do a lot of things that I can't handle. And I'm not sure it will make a difference anyway."

Strengthening the Empathic Envelope

Because parents believe they are powerless over peer influence, when a book like Judith Rich-Harris's *The Nurture Assumption* comes out, they become even more distraught. The book implied to many that parents really don't matter and that the influence of peers weighs in more heavily than what happens at home. This echoed many parents' worst nightmare. Mothers and fathers realize that it does take a whole village to raise kids—and they know how busy they and the rest of the villagers are! Feeling that the problem looms so much larger than they, parents then throw up their hands in despair. They think that their only recourse is to set limits and hold firm to the rules—at least they can show their kids who's boss.

Unfortunately, that's not enough.

Obviously, we need to give our kids guidelines and structure so that they learn how to act in the world (more about that later), but we also have to *meet* them on an emotional level. *In short, there needs to be a balance between expectations and empathy.*

How do parents and other adults achieve such a balance? To be sure, entering our children's world is not always easy—it takes courage to lay down our prejudices against Planet Youth. And it is by no means a panacea. But I can assure you, when parents *don't* make an attempt—by getting to know the music kids play, the TV and movies they watch, the celebrities they worship—it's a pretty good bet that their teenagers will continue to move farther and farther from their first-family sphere of influence.

To understand this concept, imagine a container around your family, an invisible barrier that separates you and your child from the larger culture. That's what I call the *empathic envelope*, a term I introduced a decade ago in *Parenting by Heart*, to help parents recognize the need for both consequences and compassion. The empathic envelope is made up of your values, your expectations, and your ways of spending time with your children. Family life occurs on the edges of the envelope, especially with teens who are constantly pushing, haggling, and rene-gotiating its borders.

If, in 1991, it was difficult for parents to keep the culture at bay, today it's even tougher. Now more than ever, parents need to strengthen the empathic envelope, but that doesn't mean keeping your child in a pumpkin shell. There is a way of extending the edges of the envelope to *include* the second family and, at the same time, maintain first-family values.

By definition, the empathic envelope helps parents achieve precisely the kind of balance I advocate: between expectations and empathy, authority and acceptance. You set limits, but limits only make sense if you also show compassion and understanding for your teen's world. When parents are willing to bring into the empathic envelope what their children are watching, listening to, and interested in—that is, to carve out what I call *comfort time*—teenagers know that they also can have in their first family the sense of ease and support they typically get from their second family. Moreover, kids whose parents strengthen the envelope in this way will feel held, which is exactly what teenagers need.

Creating Comfort Time

Since the '70s, when mothers began to enter the workplace in increasing numbers, childrearing books have touted the benefits of creating "quality time" with kids. This became the catchphrase of several decades, easing parents' guilt by implying that it's not how much time you spend, but what you do with kids that counts. Quality time was defined in one-on-one terms—a time to really connect with your child. The idea was to relate to each other while participating in "enriching," wholesome activities. But what looked good on paper didn't actually work as well in real life. As I wrote in 1991, "It's virtually impossible for most of us to fit so-called 'quality time' into our hectic lives."

It's even harder now.

Modern families call for a redefinition of parent-child togetherness, and it's not just because quality time has failed us. Given the strength of the second family, to reach your child, you need to share comfort time. This means changing your old approach—going from one-on-one time to embracing ways that the second family prefers to congregate—in groups and engaged with media or computers. It means bending, *but not breaking*, some of your own values about what's acceptable and what's not. And it means learning about, rather than dismissing, people, pursuits, and things that might even frighten you!

Coining the term *comfort time,* I didn't just reach into the air for an intriguing or clever phrase. Comfort *is* what kids are seeking. They've been brought up in a culture that prizes ease and convenience. Air-conditioning keeps our homes at temperate levels; delivery services make our daily chores easier; remote controls mean we never have to budge from that cozy couch in the den. Bill Gates instinctively understood this when he attributed the success of the personal computer to the fact that it ultimately allows you to get what you want when you want it.

Most of us wouldn't dream of living without modern conveniences, so why should it surprise us that teens would take this notion to the max? It's not a matter of their being spoiled; they simply *expect* and seek out comfort. It's an idea that is introduced early and reinforced often. Virtually everything kids do is motivated by the pursuit of comfort. Now-adays my adolescent balks about going to the video store, even though it's less than two minutes away. She'd rather call the local "dot.com" company, which promises to deliver virtually anything to our door in an hour or less. Even five-year-olds know they don't have to leave home to get what they want. They can order their *Pokémon, Digimon,* or Dra-gonball Z cards over the Internet. If it takes too long for a plot to get going or for kids to understand a character in a TV show or movie, click! They change the channel. If they can't tolerate the frustrations of being a beginner, adolescents quit sports or music lessons. Instead they often opt for video games—a classic example of an amusement that delivers what kids want, when they want it.

Video games and other captivating high-tech gadgets offer nonstop stimulation—which is an important feature of kids' comfort. In fact, children today are *un*comfortable when they're *not* being stimulated. As the Kaiser Foundation study demonstrated, youngsters are no longer content to simply sit in front of the TV. "Most children spend at least part of their day using more than one media at a time," the report states, noting that because of this factor it was impossible for the researchers to calculate kids' total media-use time. In other words, the average child often has a comic book open and a video game in hand while he's watching his favorite TV program. Maybe the computer is on, too!

This craving for stimulation is honed when kids are babies, and parents hang bright mobiles over the crib and strategically place flash cards near the bumpers. By two, most kids are already accustomed to TV as background noise. I've had middle school children say to me — and I've seen that it's true — "I study better with the TV on." Though it sounds counterintuitive, stimulation actually equals comfort to most modern kids.

Children's increasing need for stimulation has been documented by researchers, who have linked it with acting-out behavior. The phenomenon has long been heeded by teachers, who are painfully aware that they easily "lose" kids if what happens in their classroom is not arousing enough. And it has been paid attention to by some parents, especially if their kids have learning problems. Still, kids' need for arousal is rarely viewed as something that helps them maintain a comfort level.

Children's drive to find a comfort zone is generally not in adults' consciousness. Yet teens, in particular, splinter into peer groups precisely because they're looking for a place where they feel comfortable. Kids team up with other kids who are like them and *prefer similar modes of stimulation*. With these buddies they don't have to explain themselves. Hence, when we think of spending time with kids, it's important to respect the inescapable reality that comfort is their touchstone.

Comfort time is asking teenagers what they like to see and hear and then watching the TV program, the movie, or listening to the music *with* them. Comfort time is sitting next to your daughter while she reads the biographical information about Freddy Prinze Jr. on the Internet. Comfort time is having your son teach you how to play whatever video game currently captures his imagination and interest. Comfort time even includes occasionally going to a rock concert with your twelve-year-old.

You might be amazed: When you enter *their* world, get involved with something *they're* interested in, kids won't automatically want to exclude you simply because you're an adult. Today's teen is surprisingly receptive to spending comfort time with adults — as long as the grownup doesn't try to be someone he or she is not. Kids see right through adults who pretend to know more about a teen interest than they actually do, who act as if they like a particular rock group when they don't, or who say that something is "cool"—an adolescent character on *Grosse Pointe* getting a tattoo—when it's really offensive. Kids are also nonplussed when an adult remarks, "Hey, this sounds just like the groups I listened to in college." It's best therefore, to be honest, and certainly not to err to either extreme.

And remember: Comfort time *doesn't* include lecturing or acting like a therapist. "My parents don't get it," said Vicki, a thirteen-year-old whose folks were worried because she never talked to them. "My friends and I get turned off when older people talk to us and tell us what to do. We don't even tell *each other* what to do. My mom is constantly trying to teach me things. I wouldn't mind hearing her opinions, if she waited to be asked." What bothered Vicki the most was that her mom often commented on other kids' behavior. "That's not right—that's not her business."

I've counseled the parents of my teenage clients to put less emphasis on molding and monitoring if it's at the expense of comfort time. This is not to say that you're going to be a "pal"—a parent who is overly indulgent. This is not about catering; it's about getting to know the kids you care about better. You'll have more meaningful conversations in these groupings than you would one-on-one, so invite your kids' friends to dinner and take them on family outings. In this way, you'll get to know what's going on in your kid's world. *Then you can shape and guide.*

I've heard from successful parents in my workshops that sharing comfort time enables them to stay connected to their children even through adolescence. Indeed, comfort time is a way of helping parents change their perspective, positioning themselves to be slightly more respectful of second-family mores and values. In seeing a child's world realistically, that delicate balance, being both accepting *and* authoritative, becomes possible.

To expand the empathic envelope and to create comfort time within it, you must abandon your old ways of thinking. The process involves opening up: *your heart* (having empathy and understanding for your child and his or her friends), *your mind* (suspending judgment about kids' interests), and *your home* (making your house a place kids like to congregate, but also one that has rules).

Opening Your Heart

The empathic envelope must have *flexible* boundaries, which means, first and foremost, opening your heart. When we put up a wall of resistance around second-family interests and tenaciously hold on to our prejudices about peers, we actually close ourselves off from our children. We can't truly see our kids or hear them and, worst of all, can't *feel* them. But by being tolerant of teenagers' likes and dislikes, by welcoming and encouraging their friends, parents also fling open the door to their child's emotions—and their own.

Remember Alicia, whom you met in the last chapter—the so-called bitch? She had come to the rescue of Matt by offering to have him hang out at her house after school instead of going home to his parents who, according to him, "smoked pot too much." Alicia's mother, Cay, was initially upset to have Matt constantly underfoot. When she called me to complain, my response was, "Good—encourage it."

"But I'm afraid that this kid is going to influence Alicia," she said. "You know—if his parents are so heavily into grass, what's to say that if he isn't already smoking, he might be tempted to experiment? And then he's going to drag Alicia down with him."

I urged Cay to suspend her prejudice for a few weeks. "Cay, give yourself a chance to know who these kids are," I admonished gently. "If Alicia's bringing friends home, it's a good sign. That means that, no matter how she acts toward you, on some level she knows she can come to you. Don't blow this opportunity. You have to at least try to be respectful of her world. It's the only way to begin to narrow the gap, *and* get to know whether Alicia's in danger."

Cay, a former hippie herself, had tuned out and dropped acid in her day. Now she was afraid her daughter was on the same, or worse, track. I often hear this scenario from other parents as well. They think back to when they were kids and assume that their children are bound to rebel against them, too. "You have to put *your* experiences behind you," I advised, "and not assume that Alicia is exactly like you."

To her credit, Cay, who is a quick study, started listening to Alicia and her friends. Rather than giving in to her natural instinct to make every conversation a "teaching moment," Cay just talked to the kids when they came over. Whereas she had normally tried to pass along her philosophy of life, her experiences, and her opinions, Cay now kept her ideas to herself for a while, choosing instead to listen and observe — until she was asked.

After some time, Cay called. "You know, this Matt is really a nice kid after all. I feel for him. I just listen when he talks to me, and see how happy that makes Alicia. She'd never admit it, of course, but I know." By first opening her heart, Cay was able to start widening the empathic envelope. It was an important first step in reeling her daughter back in.

Opening Your Mind

None of this is for the faint of heart. When teenagers talk about what they're "into," our *best* response is usually boredom. The descriptions and discussions are so much more complex and elaborate than our own teen interests were. Rarely do we comprehend the intricate details of a video game or care about the labyrinthine love life of some teen idol. At *worst*, we're horrified, even disgusted. The Beatles seem like choir boys next to Marilyn Manson. As objectionable as Mick Jagger might have seemed to our parents, when your son or daughter excitedly talks about groups like Nine Inch Nails, Rage Against the Machine, or the pop star Eminem, your stomach churns.

I know mine did. A few years ago, when one teen after another came into my office mentioning such groups, I was as nonplussed as their parents. I couldn't be bothered; I was "too busy" with therapy. I was dismissive and disgusted. At one point, a fourteen-year-old girl actually asked me, "Doesn't hearing all this stuff make you scared about what's going to happen to your own kids?"

She was right. I know, of course, that "out there" my children have heard it all! Beneath my repulsion, I now realize, was also fear and the belief that, as an adult, this was *not my business, not my world*. But as teen after teen kept bringing CDs or video-game manuals to my office, I finally got the idea. They wanted me to listen.

In time, I came to see pop-culture fare, even though much of it is abhorrent, as a part of preteen and adolescent life that I simply could not ignore. I discovered that the only way to get through to certain kids was to meet them, not halfway, but actually *in* their world. When teens talked about the messages of these bands, I was skeptical of course, but I realized I had to at least know more. So, I purchased an inexpensive boom box and we listened together. I felt outraged; the music was raw, the lyrics exactly what I had anticipated: obscene, rageful, irreverent, sexist, homophobic, and horrifyingly graphic. The songs were often about incest, child abuse, self-mutilation, casual violence, and, of course, sex. It was difficult and, at first, intensely embarrassing to listen while sitting across from a passionate teenager who was just waiting to see my reaction.

Listening only strengthened my support for the rating system, advisory labels, V-chips, and any other action that gives parents a modicum of greater control. I am a firm believer in the First Amendment. But I wished and still do that the business of pop culture practiced greater self-reflection about what it offers our kids. Until that happens, however, everything is out there, it's everywhere, and we adults need to know what it is.

So I listened and learned. It surprised me that so many white kids listen to hip-hop, inspired by life in urban ghettos, and I struggled to understand why middle-class teenagers relate to the lyrics. The fact is, they do. In the second-family realm, walls have come tumbling down between races, ethnic groups, and classes—at least when it comes to music and other forms of entertainment. A sampling from 2 Live Crew, an understandably controversial rap group, speaks to the "deal with it" message kids are telling us about the second family:

> *Now let me break it on down and tell the story*
> *When they say "2 Live," your mama gets worried*
> *When they speak of us, the negative get mentioned*

But we don't care; thanks for your attention
An underground sound, talkin' shit off the street
That Ghetto Style with a hard-ass beat
Our explicit lyrics tells it like it is
If you don't like what I'm saying, get the fuck outta here!

Despite my fear and loathing, I began to listen more closely to songs spanning the continuum—pop, heavy metal, rock, rap, alternative, industrial—and to discuss with my young wards what drew them in. I saw that just as Dylan spoke what was in my heart in the '60s, some lyrics of these songs give voice to a generation that often feels pain unknown to the adults in their lives. More important, once I was actually willing to listen to their music, even as we argued over the destructive messages of their lyrics, teenagers trusted me more. In turn, they allowed me a fuller glimpse into their universe.

Opening my mind to the second family in this way was the beginning of a major shift in my practice. In fact, among my client population, I could almost always tell how much danger a child was in by his or her parents' familiarity with the teen culture. Recognizing that you can't effectively fight what you don't know, I began to urge parents and other adults to open their eyes and ears. My articles and workshops on these issues triggered a tremendous response. Mental-health practitioners, teachers, guidance counselors, even clergy, reacted to the possibility of establishing traction with *their* lost clients, too. Of course, among those professionals are many parents who are dealing with teen-related problems at home.

Not surprisingly, I underwent a similar metamorphosis in my own family, although our kids' taste (to date) runs toward milder fare. When my daughter, then eleven, began to watch *Party of Five* a few years ago, I saw how important the show was to her. She finished her homework without urging on Wednesday evenings, and when the clock struck nine, everything else came to a stop. Curious, I started watching the show with her. To my surprise, I found it quite compelling. The acting was good, and the show was tackling very sensitive issues. Suddenly, we were talking for hours about the various characters and their plot lines— would Claudia really stop playing the violin because she wanted to be popular, would Charlie and Kirsten ever get back together, would Sara lose her virginity? That I took such questions seriously opened up countless other avenues of discussion about dating, substance abuse, sex. Suddenly, we weren't in such different worlds anymore.

Judd, a college professor, experienced similar strengthening of the empathic envelope when he became willing to explore the world of wrestling with his stepson, Tyler, who was totally captivated by the matches. Wrestling violated everything this gentle man believed in and valued. "They call it 'action entertainment,' " Judd told me, "but I see it as violent, fascistic, and misogynistic." All the same, he pushed past his own feelings in order to connect with Tyler. Going to matches with his stepson was not only a way of developing a relationship with Tyler, whom Judd had only come to know in his early teens—a difficult prospect for any stepparent—but it also helped bridge the adult/teen gap. Judd didn't go to many matches, nor did he rave about the sport when he did. He never gave up his own beliefs. But by showing some interest, his actions said to Tyler, "I'm taking time to get to know you." Their subsequent discussions about various wrestlers, whom the boy liked or didn't, led to other conversations. Tyler started talking about *his* world, confiding in Judd what he hadn't felt comfortable admitting to his mother: he had been having trouble standing up to some of the more cruel boys at school. Through this simple act of showing an interest in wrestling, Judd strengthened his capacity for empathy, which immediately improved his relationship with Tyler.

Opening Your Home

A natural by-product of opening your heart and mind is to welcome your child's friends into your home. It often happens spontaneously, but it's also important to *keep an eye out for opportune moments*— and seize them. When I started watching *Party of Five* with Leah, word spread among her friends. Soon kids were gravitating to our house on Wednesdays when the show came on. Over the years, we moved on to *Dawson's Creek, Friends, Popular,* and *Caitlin's Way,* but the ritual of having friends over for dinner and a favorite TV show persisted. Our house became one where kids could have an "intelligent discussion" about these programs—TV fare that some parents considered junk.

All the same, I have vivid and tender memories of my wife and I talking with girls in Leah's core group, asking them which of the female characters on *Friends* they'd most like to be, which boy they'd most like to date. By listening to them, we not only gained insight into each kid—including our own daughter—we were also able to connect with them on a meaningful level.

The interactions with Leah and her friends altered me as well, too, because I realized how aware and how sophisticated these girls were about life. They knew far more than I did at their age. For instance, when we watched the speed-boat scene on *Dawson's Creek* (see page 37) with its clear intimation of oral sex, rather than the girls running out of the room in embarrassment as I'd have done with my folks, the three of them started jeering and talking back to the screen.

That they were willing to watch this with my wife, and to talk about what rang true and what didn't, made me push past my own embarrassment. If twelve-year-olds could be this open about sexual matters, I knew I had better get involved in the conversation. Our bold venturing into this new territory ultimately elevated my relationship with Leah. Her friends knew I respected their opinions and didn't think that "their show" was stupid or irrelevant. I had opened myself to them, so they gave me a chance, too.

Some parents are naturally good with teenagers and have a relatively easy time making their house a drop-in center for the whole second family. Others have to work at it. But the end result is almost always the same: when your child's friends want to be with you, *your child* becomes more receptive to your guidance as well.

The Youngs, a family I knew, seemed to handle this effortlessly. Starting in junior high, their house became a hotel for six to eight kids at a time. Dora and Tom weren't the richest people, didn't have the nicest house, didn't even own a big entertainment center. So, what was their secret?

Their campaign began the summer before Kirk entered seventh grade. "Now that you're getting ready for junior high," they told him, "we want to help you make your room into a place where you and your friends can hang out. But we need your help." Together, the three of them went through Kirk's things and got rid of a lot of clutter. They built shelves and bunk beds to maximize the space, and finally gave the room a new paint job—deep purple, a color neither of the parents would have chosen!

The new arrangement created space for comfort time without Dora and Tom having to compromise their standards. Whenever Kirk brought his friends around, Mom and Dad wisecracked with them, but they always acted like parents, not buddies. As a result, everyone loved to meet and sleep over at the Youngs' house. It didn't hurt that the refrigerator was always well-stocked—with junk *and* healthier food.

Dora also told Kirk's friends what she expected of them: No smoking. When you take food out of the refrigerator and don't finish it, rewrap what's left and put it back. Clean the counter after eating. If it's raining heavily, remove your shoes at the door. In this way, the Youngs let the kids know that the adults were in charge but, at the same time, nurtured them. Whoever came to the house had to call his parents and let them know where he was—that was the price of admission. Dora and Tom were never in the kids' faces; they stayed in the next room but every once in a while popped in to say hello. While a few of Kirk's friends clung to the anonymity of hanging out in his room, more often, the kids would wander into the kitchen or living room and start up conversations with his mom or dad. It was all very easy and organic. Most important, the Youngs always knew where their son was and what he was up to.

The Youngs' secret, then, was their ability to maintain that tricky balance, setting limits yet also knowing when to hold back. They had clear expectations of their son and his friends, but also a genuine interest in what these youngsters did and thought. I'm not surprised that even now, some ten years later, their son Kirk, a college graduate, *still* brings other kids over during the holidays.

I learned from watching Dora and Tom that to make your house into a place kids flock to, one must be a parental presence, communicating directly with your child's friends. By telling the other boys what she expected, Dora made sure everyone knew the score, which kept her son from feeling as if he was in the middle. Imagine what a burden it is for a teen to be responsible for making friends conform to his parents' rules. It's like a child of divorce caught between warring parties, but here a child would feel torn between his two "families," the one at home and the one out there.

The Surprising By-products of Reaching Out

Of course, miracles don't happen merely because parents open their hearts, minds, and homes. But I've always seen a difference, sometimes subtle, sometimes mind-boggling. The kids drift toward adults, fear them less, welcome them more. The adults lose their rigidity, their resentment, and, most important, the overriding sense of fear that goes with the territory of parenting today. What follows are some real-life stories of ways in which parents, some of whose kids you've already met in these pages, have been able to open themselves up to their childrens' second families. Not all stories turn out so well; but for a moment it is helpful to hear about some positive experiences—and to learn from them.

Betsy and Henry: Allowing for Comfort Time

Betsy and Henry, parents of Billy, the "amoral slacker" you met in the last chapter (page 56), were vehemently *not* interested in any of their son's second-family pursuits. As it was, they were appalled by his permanent state of dishevelment, his hair, and his pierced body parts. Naturally, their disgust extended to the music he listened to and the video games he played, which they thought were downright horrifying. My job was to help them understand the notion of comfort time, which meant approaching Billy's world. I told them they had to develop a modicum of patience and empathy, which would allow them to get past their own visceral response to their son's interests. At my urging, I suggested to Betsy and Henry that they actually *listen*, instead of spontaneously reject, Rage Against the Machine, which was one of Billy's favorite groups. They didn't change their mind about the music, but the experience at least opened them up to the idea that the lyrics had significance to their son and that the group stood for something in his eyes.

In this and other cases, a balance was achieved on two levels: *When his parents showed an interest in his world, Billy let them in, which, in turn, allowed Betsy and Henry to both know their son and better guide him.* Also, Billy became more willing to enter his parents' world. Prior to this point, although Billy had benefited greatly from his father's success, he knew nothing about what the man, a financial analyst, actually did. Opening up to his son, Dad started talking more concretely about his business and the workings of the stock market, which Billy found instantly intriguing. Just as Henry was coming to see what Billy's day-to-day world was like, his son began to see him as a real person, too — in fact, as someone who could teach him more about the world of investing.

Billy's relationship with his mother also changed. When she read the Rage Against the Machine *Battle of Los Angeles* album liner notes, Betsy learned, to her surprise, that the group urged fans to contribute to a number of charities, which she also supported. Suddenly, mother and son's discussions moved from her talking *at* Billy to genuinely sharing with him why she had passion for those charities. In turn, Billy actually listened to her. She, too, became less of a cardboard figure in his eyes. As it turned out, the chasm between the two generations shrank a bit. Adults and teens weren't so absolutely different from each other as each had previously believed.

Marty: Meeting on His Son's Turf

Harrison, a thirteen-year-old, was sent to me initially because he was an outcast. He had few friends at school except for the two or three boys he played video games with, an activity that absorbed up to five or six hours of his day. When Harrison wasn't playing the games himself, he fantasized about elaborate worlds populated by media-inspired super-heroes. His schoolwork was suffering, but that wasn't everyone's greatest concern. Superficially at least, if ever there was a kid who fit the profile of loner-outcast, he seemed to be it.

Knowing that I had to meet Harrison on *his* turf, I asked him to lead me into the stupifying world of violent video games. Once I showed an interest, Harrison responded. Like many other kids, he eagerly brought in huge volumes containing the official guidelines for the games he was involved with. Here was a kid who had problems concentrating on schoolwork, yet he was able to pore through these manuals, keep the rules straight, and remember what was happening in each world. Ad-mittedly, my first reaction was similar to my response to rap artists. It was easy to see how being involved in these violent games could, if a teen was predisposed, prompt aggression. The sentiment found in the manuals could be paraphrased as: *In the future world, there is nothing but chaos, pain, and death.* I asked Harrison, "Why are you interested in this?"

"I know this sounds crazy," he replied, "but by fantasizing about my worlds, I'm learning how to be a little more patient. It helps me to focus and teaches me to think."

"What about the violence?" I asked.

"It's only pretend," he said, as if that were obvious. "And the real world *is* about good and evil, isn't it?"

I wondered to myself, *Is this just an excuse to make these games seem palatable to adults?* But Harrison's relationships at home *did* start to improve.

After working with him for a few weeks, I called his father in to report on our progress and urged Dad to open up his heart and mind and at least see what these games and these worlds were about. Marty, who was quite conservative and intellectual, was aghast at the mere thought.

I admitted to Marty, "When Harrison first brought his rule books in, I was stunned, too. I was also appalled at the terror and horrific chaos of the dark world that these games portray. But it was through talking about this stuff—who played with him, who were his friends, who stuck by him—that Harrison began to open up to me."

Marty reluctantly said he and his wife would try to be a bit more receptive. There was no overnight transformation on either parents' or child's part, but within five or six months, the darkness in their house lifted. Both the adults and the teenager were starting to change. Harrison talked to his parents more, even discussing his fantasy worlds. The more candid he was with his parents, the *less* time he spent totally obsessed with action games. Over time, his parents became increasingly open, not just to their son's interests, but also to his friends. At one point, they threw a party for a whole group of Harrison's friends. Marty admitted that he hadn't been this happy with Harrison since he was five or six years old—the last time he felt like he really knew the boy.

Cay: Learning How to Keep the Balance

A similar transformation happened with Alicia and her mom. (See pages 59 and 85.) It was a slow process, though, as it usually is; change doesn't happen at once, but success builds on success. By first opening her heart, and learning how not to prejudge a situation, Cay became so much better at holding back her opinion that other kids began showing up at her house, too. Cay didn't keep telling them to turn the music down; she listened to it. In time, instead of always holing up in Alicia's room, the kids started seeking out Cay. Cay began to ask them to stay for dinner. She became such a good sounding board that eventually her own daughter trusted her enough to admit there was a boy—Michael— that she had a crush on.

"I held my breath, not believing she'd actually confide in me," Cay recalls. This wise mom had learned that she didn't have to be her daughter's therapist. She certainly wasn't mute when Alicia's friends were around, but she also didn't push, teach, or remind. The only time she stepped in was when something was literally dangerous, for example, a child trying to drive while under the influence.

One night, Alicia brought Michael home to dinner. Later, she stunned her mother by actually asking her opinion: "Is it okay for me to hook up with Michael even though I've been with Jeremy?" That sounded harmless enough, but then Alicia started telling Cay what she meant by "hooking up" and what other kids were doing at parties: hand jobs in sixth grade and oral sex in junior high. Managing to keep her anxiety at bay, Cay at least was able to listen. "Believe me, I thought to myself, *do I really want to know this*? Still, it opened a door, and I knew that this was not the time for me to be harshly judgmental."

Cay was at least able to say clearly—and her daughter actually listened—that such behavior was dangerous and unacceptable. In addition, whatever Alicia did with boys on weekends, Cay explained, she would have to answer for during the week when she found herself sitting next to these same guys in class. Therefore, Mom suggested that Alicia try to think through her behavior before acting on her impulses. Cay also pointed out a painful reality: word among teenagers spreads quickly. A girl can easily get reputation for being a "slut," as Alicia had already seen happen to some other girls at school. Is that what she wanted for herself? In Cay's talk she also let Alicia know, "At your age, I don't believe it's right for girls to go that far. Later is better." (As the father of a teen, I understood completely when Cay also admitted, "Actually, I *wanted* to tell her that *never* was better!")

Here again was that important balance: although Cay was clearly still the parent, the one who made the rules and enforced them, she was also accepting, empathic, and realistic. As a result, Alicia was more willing to listen to what she had to say. Unlike many of her junior high school friends, Alicia *has* waited. Although I'm certain that at some point soon, she will become more sexually active, for now at least, feeling her mother's support and understanding no doubt strengthens Alicia's resolve.

In the weeks that followed these initial talks, Alicia even garnered the courage to share a dark secret with her mother that she had been afraid to talk about: many years earlier, an older cousin had molested her. Because it was so hard for her to explain how she felt, she offered to play one of Korn's songs for her mother. In the past, Cay might have dismissed her daughter's suggestion, not wanting to hear such raw music. But now, having new understanding and compassion for her daughter's world, she listened intently to the lyrics. The song, entitled "Daddy," told of an "innocent child" raped by her father. She is hurt; she feels dirty; she screams, and yet no one comes to her rescue. At the end of the verse, the girl protests, "I am not a liar." Hearing the words to Korn's song, Cay understood that although she might have not liked the foul language or the abject vulgarity, the situation and the feelings the songwriters expressed gave voice to the shame Alicia had harbored all those years.

Cay bubbled over with enthusiasm and gratitude when she related these stories. She had discovered, to paraphrase Freud, "The Royal Road"—not to her child's unconscious, but to Alicia's core self. Finally, she and her daughter were able to have the realistic, open-hearted discussions that had previously been reserved only for the second family and TV shows. From these discussions she could help her daughter make smarter choices.

Marsha and John: Opening Up

Recall from the previous chapter (page 60) that Tony's parents, Marsha and John, thought he was arrogant and disconnected. Who could blame them? Tony regularly harangued them by saying such things as, "You're useless to me" and "The only thing I care about is the money you give me to buy clothes." They knew that their son had lots of friends, but they dismissed those relationships as unimportant. In fact, Tony's peer network threatened them. Even worse, Marsha had a tendency toward lashing out verbally. And on several occasions she felt so hurt and rejected by Tony that she snapped, screaming obscenities and saying things like: "You're a loser." "You're a wimp." "I wish I'd never had you!"—all in the guise of "reaching" her son.

At my urging, both parents began to show Tony that they respected his other relationships. Marsha, who worked at home, encouraged him to invite kids over. She took a casual interest in what the kids did and talked about. The more Mom got to know Tony, the less inclined she was to employ verbal insults as a means of controlling her son. John, who was a sound technician, invited Tony's gang to come backstage after one of his productions. As John felt less pushed away by his son, less an object of contempt, he occasionally offered to chauffeur Tony's friends to parties.

Nothing dramatic happened in Tony's family—their home didn't suddenly become a warm, cozy haven for teenagers. In fact, Tony only occasionally brought friends over—he still didn't trust his mom or dad not to explode. But the atmosphere changed. The aggression stopped. And Tony's parents gradually began to see another side of their son. He had a way of cutting through the details and the drama and, in doing so, often helped other kids solve their problems. The more his parents knew and understood their son's friendships, the less disconnected he acted toward them. For the last year there have been no aggressive outbursts in their home.

Maria: Pushing Past Her Own Distaste

Maria, a Latina from a conservative background, was appalled when I suggested that rather than fight with her thirteen-year-old daughter, Anna, about going to a Hole concert, she join her. Initially, Maria couldn't even bear to say the name of the group. She knew little of Courtney Love, who was its lead singer, but the little she knew scared and sickened her. She was sure that these young women were degrading themselves, parading on the stage as they did; and she imagined her own daughter descending into depravity. But in the name of deepening the bond with Anna, who had become increasingly distrustful of adults, Maria agreed to take the plunge.

Like most parents, Maria *was* shocked by the anger and sheer intensity of the crowd, the smell of marijuana everywhere. She certainly didn't walk away humming the music or eager to buy Hole's Greatest Hits. But she realized that she didn't have to regard her daughter's taste as a personal assault against her mothering. Calming down, Maria could even begin to see that the singers were not mere sex objects as she had feared. They had made their own choices and were asserting their power in the world. Naturally, many of the songs referred obliquely to Kurt Cobain's suicide. But they also urged their fans to stand up for themselves, rather than blindly conform to other people's expectations.

Though she was still put off by the words, Maria at least had something to talk about with Anna. She recognized the music when Anna played the latest Hole CD or when one of the group's songs came on the radio. Anna didn't expect Mom to embrace her music, but Maria's willingness to learn earned her daughter's respect and trust. The two "strangers" began to talk. And Mom's new mind-set opened up avenues neither expected. For one thing, Maria became more assertive herself. She was less embarrassed about talking to Anna's teachers. She even became a role model for parents, who were understandably shocked when she told them she attended a hard rock concert. When she explained her motives, though, other adults, even teachers, took notice.

Sensing her mother's newfound receptivity, Anna was willing to discuss difficult issues. For the first time, this heretofore arms-length daughter even sought her mother's help. She knew some kids would be drinking heavily and smoking pot at a party she had been invited to, and she actually asked if Mom could help her figure out how to handle the situation.

Olivia: Taking a Second Look

In several other instances, I've seen parents' willingness to embrace kids spill over into other families. For example, Billy, whose mom had regular potluck dinners for his friends, started dating Moira, a girl in New Jersey whom he met at camp: a good student, a jock, and a very responsible young woman. When he invited her to spend a weekend at his parents' apartment in New York, Moira's mother, Olivia, had had mixed feelings about her daughter getting involved with this kid from Manhattan, who was a bit too hip for Mom's liking. At first, she said "no." But in the face of Moira's incessant begging, against her better judgment, she gave in.

When Olivia heard what Billy's home was like, her negative attitude toward him began to change. Moira told her about Dorothy's Friday-night cooking ritual and enthused over how much fun she'd had cooking with Billy's mom and his friends. She decided to return the favor and invited Billy to spend the weekend with them. The three of them baked together for two days, making brownies—which they then delivered to a local hospital.

Once they involved Billy in their home life and were able to observe firsthand how he acted toward Moira, the parents finally softened toward this boy, whom they'd seen as a threat. Despite his "gangsta" look, they realized he was quite sweet and smart. Moira's father, who was interested in stereo equipment, discovered that Billy was also a font of information about electronics. What could have evolved into a chronic power struggle with their daughter turned into a mostly worthwhile experience for both the adults and the teens.

Laura and Maxine: Mothers Joining Forces

Nick's mother, Laura, felt excluded from the daily life of her fifteen-year-old son, who spent many afternoons at other kids' houses, and most weekend nights hanging out with his crew. He rarely brought friends home, hardly mentioned where he was going, and never told Mom about the details of his days. Meanwhile, his grades were slipping, and Laura was convinced, though without hard evidence, that his friends were "smoking up" quite a lot. She suspected, too, that Nick had begun hooking up with Emma, one of the girls in his group. But all of this was based on conjecture.

Not much would have changed if Laura hadn't moved out of her own isolation. Nick clearly wasn't going to open up to his mother without some kind of prodding. But, first, she had to learn more about Nick's world. There might be a chance of her finding out some concrete information about him from Emma's mother, Maxine. Since she knew Maxine casually from parent-teacher nights—Emma and Nick had been in the same school for several years—I encouraged Laura to reach out to her. A bit nervous and afraid of being "intrusive," Laura nevertheless took my suggestion.

"Hi," she said to Maxine over the phone, "we don't really know each other very well, but I thought it might be a good idea for the two of us to get together over tea or coffee and talk. I suspect our kids have become quite close." To Laura's relief, Maxine welcomed the call. At their initial meeting, Maxine was friendly and forthright, spilling all she knew about the kids. She admitted that her daughter had kept her in the dark, too.

As it turned out, the mothers began speaking frequently and found strength in this alliance of two adults who had common concerns about second-family behavior. Together, they opened their hearts, minds, and homes. As the two women became closer, they planned family dinners, which naturally included their teenagers. Laura and Maxine got to know Nick and Emma as a "couple" and came to support the relationship for the empathy, friendship, and even protection the kids offered each other. Nick and Emma didn't admit it to either mother, but it was clear from their eagerness to plan the next family outing that they enjoyed their mothers' warmth and acceptance. Even more telling, the two of them willingly started to hang out at home, rather than constantly running out to meet their friends.

■

The bottom line is that an involved, open-minded adult, who doesn't ram ideas down kids' throats, is someone teens turn to when the chips are down. An empathic parent or teacher is listened to because he or she doesn't have a knee-jerk reaction to second-family fare—the music, the movies, or the other interests kids cultivate. These adults learn about such things, know what the kids are talking about, and therefore can help young people make better decisions. When teens rail against a rule or feel disappointed because they're not allowed to attend a concert or an unsupervised party, parents can understand the child's reaction and are less likely to take it personally—or to cave in.

Like the successful teachers, coaches, counselors, and clergy I've met, such parents adeptly walk that fine line between being a presence in a child's life and offering privacy. They constantly strive for a balance between expectation and empathy, between laying down rules for children and respecting the world they inhabit, between nurturing and just saying "no." They recognize that the second family is here to stay and that it's better to deal with it realistically than to ignore it. Admittedly, it's often hard to know when to step in, when to hold back. The next chapter looks at how wise parents and other adults responsible for children's welfare cope with the everyday dilemmas that life with teenagers inevitably brings.

5

"Don't Let Me Slip Away"

Lying and the Empathic Envelope

In the face of teenagers' lying and other outrageous acts of self-preservation, the best intentioned and most conscientious adults are both confused and frightened. They often labor under misconceptions about teens' motives and overestimate kids' comprehension of right and wrong. To connect with kids, adults have to be realistic, to see past the lies, and, in this way, strike a balance between expectations and empathy.

Move Over, Pinocchio

Not all stories end as harmoniously as the ones I just described in the last chapter. The situation is often complicated by adults who are unable to be more open and kids who are unwilling to be honest about their second-family lives. In fact, teen lying is so pervasive, many of today's adolescents make the boy with the long nose look like a novice.

Andrea, cute as a button, articulate, seemingly an open book, was referred to me because she was mildly anxious about starting junior high and handling a different kind of social life. Months into our sessions, I found out that not only had this Best Little Girl in the World been cheating on tests, she was the ringleader of a gang who had managed to pilfer the exams beforehand. When I learned this, I was devastated. It was as if I had been standing on a high precipice and suddenly looked down. My stomach dropped. How could this sweet child come to my office week after week without betraying her double life? Not once did I even suspect that she could be lying.

Roy took his parents by surprise in much the same way. Because of a minor skirmish with another boy at school, the principal suspended him for a day and his parents grounded him for the weekend. Roy was utterly contrite; he apologized profusely to his folks, swore it wouldn't happen again. He also assured them that he deserved the punishment they had meted out.

That night, Mom and Dad went out for dinner, and Roy promptly sneaked out of the house to go to an unsupervised party where alcohol and marijuana were flowing freely. If caught, Roy faced an even longer-term grounding; but those consequences apparently only sharpened his resolve to plan well. He took the phone off the hook, which gave him a ready alibi. (He later admitted to me, "I'd have told them I was on-line when they called.") Roy timed his return perfectly but also made sure several kids were in on his plan as backup. When his parents got home, they were none the wiser. Only by chance did they discover the truth when, a few days later, a friend casually mentioned her daughter seeing Roy at a party over the weekend. They were horrified that their son had lied—and even more astounded that he had lied so well.

The kids who scare me the most are the ones whose misdeeds take adults completely by surprise. In a family of two sisters, for example, Gabby was labeled the mischief-maker, her younger sister Annette, the good one. All of the parents' punishment, lectures, and surveillance were concentrated on Gabby. Everyone, including me, assumed Annette was an angel. The reality was that at thirteen, Annette was smoking nearly a half a pack of cigarettes a day and was already having sex with several different boys. But because she was able to give vague answers and tell half stories, omitting anything that might incriminate her, no one had a clue.

Teens' shocking ease with lying even extends to ordinarily revered figures, such as clergymen. A priest told me that one Sunday morning, he noticed a cloud of smoke behind the rectory. Investigating further, he discovered a group of teenagers from this year's confirmation class. At that point, not a cigarette was in sight. All that remained was a pungent, sweet odor in the air.

"What's going on here?" he demanded of the group.

"Oh, nothing, Father," said a straight-faced Yvonne, who happened to be one of the best students in the class. "We were just taking a break."

"There was some snickering and smirking," Father Carter recalls, "but most of the kids looked innocent and even annoyed that an adult might question them."

After years of hearing other adults' shock and disbelief—years, I also have to admit, of sometimes playing the fool to *my* young minions—I got tired of feeling gullible and humiliated. Time and again, the cherub sitting across from me would so effectively pull the wool over the adult world, I finally realized that the teenagers I was trying to reach were not like any kids I'd ever seen.

What's So Bad (or New) About Teen Lying?

Lying is one of the greatest everyday threats to the empathic envelope. It is symptomatic of the more subtle ways that kids stray outside the edges of the envelope and, little by little, slip beyond the sphere of adult influence. Children who lie to parents or other adults and get away with it begin to have contempt for grownups.

Of course, adolescents have always lied to their elders. We all did it once, if not hundreds of times. We've all hatched schemes to deceive hapless parents. It was a way of asserting our independence—of outsmarting the oppressive adult establishment. At the same time, though, most of us usually felt some guilt or at least a bit of conflict. We often were nervous about our deceptions. We also occasionally got caught because we left traces and clues. In fact, the conventional wisdom had it that we "wanted to get caught." Chronic lying was a way of crying out for attention and help.

Not so with today's teens. Most of the time their lies are *not* a cry for help, *not* about rebellion, *not* about anger, and *not* about the thrill of getting over on adults. Kids lie, above all else, to protect their fun and freedom, which, these days, means their *comfort*. They lie because they want to stay on-line, go to parties, watch as much TV and play video games as long as they want, do their homework how and when they want to do it.

Lying is such an everyday tactic of self-preservation that when teenagers *don't* lie they almost feel self-righteous. Keith, a fourteen-year-old boy from Rhode Island, *tells* — not asks — his mother that on New Year's Eve he's going out with "just the boys." He and his buddies, he adds, will light a bonfire and sleep on the beach (in the dead of winter, mind you). Paula, a fine, upstanding mother who cares deeply about her son and tries desperately to stay connected to him, dies a thousand deaths as Keith spins out his plan. She tries to keep an even voice as she asks, "Is any adult going to be there?"

"Stop grilling me!" Keith shoots back angrily. "At least *I'm* not hiding what I'm planning to do. The other kids aren't even telling their parents. I should have just lied to you."

Most modern adolescents don't feel the slightest guilt about lying because to them, it's not a moral issue — it's simply a matter of getting what they want — and everybody does it anyway. For the same reasons, many of the kids I've spoken with feel absolutely no remorse afterward. Freed of this somewhat old-fashioned baggage — guilt or remorse — our teenagers are able to spin the most seamless and sometimes intricate tales without so much as blinking.

When I began to understand that adolescents saw deception as a way of protecting freedom and comfort, rather than impose guilt where none existed or to interpret some type of moral deficit, I was able to understand teenagers' lying for what it was: a dangerous distancer. Each successful lie bores another hole in the empathic envelope, because teenagers not only look down upon gullible grownups who buy their stories, it's further proof to them that adults don't have a clue about who they really are.

Ian crystallized this phenomenon. At fourteen, Ian was an everyday pot smoker. His parents didn't remotely suspect what their son was doing until, one day, clearing the table for dinner, his mother, Carol, accidentally overturned his backpack to witness an amazing array of drug paraphernalia spilling out.

Confronted, Ian offered a story — actually, a series of stories — in his own defense. Yes, he had tried it once, but he didn't like it and swore never to do it again. This wasn't his pot. He was only holding the marijuana for a friend. Well, actually he was trying to help the friend *stop* (a nice touch). And, oh, by the way, he was also doing a report for school on the dangers of marijuana.

A few months after the incident, Ian casually remarked, "I can tell my parents anything I want to tell them. And because they love me and want to believe me, they will." Just in case I didn't get his point, he then clarified, "Like if we were standing in front of a lake and I told them we were at the ocean, I'll bet in a few minutes I could make them doubt what they were seeing."

I've seen the same glib confidence in other kids. In fact, I remember two fourteen-year-olds, seemingly quite different from each other—Suze, a sassy girl from the suburbs, a "virgin" who belonged to the oral/anal sex club mentioned earlier (page 14), and Schuyler, a quiet, unassuming boy who also belonged to this exclusive sex group. Both casually mentioned to me that they regularly sneaked out of the house between *two and five in the morning* to be with their crowd, hanging out, smoking and drinking, hooking up. Like Roy, both these kids always timed it perfectly, and their parents never suspected anything. It wasn't a big deal to either of them. And in their telling of these exploits, I could hear no anxiety, only the sound of disdain for their clueless parents.

It's not only the specifics of these stories that matter, or whether the lies are innocent fibs or chronic deceptions, connected to cheating or schoolwork, to drinking or drugs or sexual behavior. It's the fact that the parents *are totally in the dark.* Such was the case with a band of nine-year-olds who regularly sneaked down to the basement to watch porn on cable. What's noteworthy here is not that nine-years-olds would watch porn and create an elaborate subterfuge in order to throw their parents off—that's a given in our day and age. The disturbing part is that although virtually every kid in the neighborhood, participant or not, was aware of what was going on, not one parent got past the kids' cover-up.

In many cases, believing that their children are "good kids," parents neither check their kids' alibis nor look for clues. The danger is that the more their kids "get away with it," the more their children literally get away from them. Moving further and further into the second family, kids become even more proficient at lying to all adults, the cycle of contempt escalates, and the empathic envelope gets progressively weaker.

Lying Styles

You can't stop teenagers from lying, but you don't have to be a floundering rube in the face of kids' deceptions. In other words, to secure the empathic envelope and to stay connected, adults need to be smarter than teenagers think they are. First, accept the fact that children will, at some time, lie to you and not suffer an ounce of guilt about it. Second, pay attention: whether you're a parent, teacher, counselor, or anyone who deals with kids, become aware of a child's modus operandi. Teenagers have shown me that they favor particular patterns of deception—a lying "style," if you will—that is the sum of three factors: their inherent traits, whatever they've picked up from the media, and their parents' vulnerabilities.

Fast talkers are blessed with silver tongues. They not only talk at a rapid pace, they're good at double-talk. Parents may at first be proud of their children—at how clever they are. But fast talkers are experts at catching parents and other adults off-guard. They make requests at the most harried moments—as a parent is walking out the door or a teacher is putting the finishing touches on an important project. Fast talkers have perfect timing, too; they never ask permission in advance and always press for an answer NOW! They wait until Friday afternoon to mention a Friday-night party. They often *announce* their plans, rather than ask parents or teachers for permission. Busy adults often find it easier to go along with them. And if they don't, these teenagers are adept at talking them out of, or making them doubt, their own instinctively correct reaction to say "no."

Slow talkers frequently have problems expressing themselves; sometimes, they have difficulty with language processing, such as word retrieval. But these deficits are used to their advantage. Parents, not realizing that some kids may be slow in school but much faster when it comes to excuses, are caught off-guard. This gives a slow talker even more of an edge. Also, when children have trouble in school, parents and even some teachers are reluctant to grill or press for further details, because they fear that it will inhibit the child or make him feel humiliated. When adults demand an explanation, slow talkers develop selective hearing, thereby giving themselves more time to hone a response. You might ask, "Where were you on Friday night?" and you'll get, "Huh?" When you repeat the question, she does too: "Where *was* I?" Slow talkers purposefully linger like this, in order to construct a perfect alibi. As one "slow" thirteen-year-old explained to me, "I go over a mental checklist: Does this story make sense? Is it believable? Am I getting my friends busted?"

Dudes (and dames) of distraction are skilled at machinations previously associated with sociopaths. They're so good at acting innocent, weaving stories with vivid details, planning elaborate schemes, and throwing adults off course, that it's hard to believe they're just ordinary kids. Remember our secret pot smoker, Ian? Before his mother discovered the paraphernalia in his backpack, to cover up his smoking, he carefully planted and sowed seeds of doubt. At the dinner table, he openly criticized dopers at school. Ian figured that his mother wouldn't suspect him of doing something he so disdained. He was right. Using similar tactics, fourteen-year-old Heide made sure she threw in a lot of extraneous details when her parents asked questions. She'd tell them what kind of house she'd been visiting, the furnishings, their animals, what the parents did for a living—all the while omitting facts she knew would get her in trouble: no adults were present and fifteen of her closest friends were skinny-dipping and hooking up in the above-ground pool. In both Ian's and Heide's situations, the details were convincing enough to satisfy parents who essentially want to see the best in their kids.

Confessors own up to a lesser crime, so as to throw adults off. Or, they suggest their own punishment, giving Mom and Dad the impression that they are appropriately remorseful. Suze, our sassy girl from the suburbs, often walked in fifteen minutes to a half hour later than her curfew, but just as her parents were about to react, she invariably announced, "I know I'm a little late. I'm so sorry. I promise I'll get up early all week to walk Fluffy." Her parents didn't add up the little inconsistencies in her story. Meanwhile, each time she deluded her folks, it was further proof to Suze of their ineptitude. Her disdain mounted and so did the distance between Suze and her folks. Not surprisingly, her dangerous behavior—vodka after school, for example—increased, too.

Pledgers give their word and mean it . . . at that moment. The road to disconnection is paved with these kids' good intentions. "Yes, I'll call you when I get there." "Sure, I'll be home at nine sharp." "You bet I'll hand in that term paper by Friday." Adults believe the pledger every time, and just about every time he or she breaks the vow. But always with a good reason: "I forgot." "There wasn't a phone there." "The bus didn't come on time." "Nora's dad didn't pick us up and we had to walk." "I put the paper in the wrong teacher's box." Even when she gets caught—say, her parents call on her beeper asking why she hasn't checked in—an excuse is ready: "I was just about to call you." Parents buy the rationalizations because pledgers are so sincere—and the cycle of deceit continues.

Litigators are budding attorneys. Even as four year olds, they argued in a way that can put their parents, and savvy teachers, on the defensive. By adolescence, their skills are finely tuned. Litigators manage to turn a situation around in a way that makes *them* the aggrieved party. Consider Austin, a very "good" kid, a straight-A student who'd never been in trouble. On the eve of her graduation, when the police in her small town in Pennsylvania responded to a complaint about an unsupervised keg party and hauled the partygoers into the police station, she was among them. Her parents, who had no idea where their daughter had been that evening, came to pick her up, only to find Austin outraged.

Despite the fact that fifty kids were "shot-drinking," many puking and/ or in various states of undress, one trying to hot-wire a luxury car parked in the driveway, Austin demanded, "What right did the cops have to trespass on private property?" as if she was arguing in front of the Supreme Court. Austin's refusal (actually, it was her inability, as I'll later explain on page 115) to accept any responsibility and to play the aggrieved party eventually bothered her parents even more than the wild scene the cops had discovered.

Plotters think like chess players, several steps ahead. Typically, they are among the more intelligent teens who tend to be underachievers at school. Plotters are able to come up with intricate schemes that often involve their peers and include multiple alibis. Steven, the boy who traveled some three thousand miles to see his girlfriend, enlisted the help of not one but several friends who agreed to cover for him. If Mom or Dad called, the friend would say, "He's in the shower," or "He just left," and then they'd beep Steven, who'd call his unsuspecting parents to "check in." After all, here was a bright kid who was a goof-off at school. They'd never imagine that he could be that organized or pay so much attention to detail.

■

You may recognize children you know in one of the foregoing sketches. Generally, teens do favor a particular style, or they may combine two. A good strategy is to pay closer attention to a child's explanations and rationalizations. You'll probably begin to notice certain ways of talking, types of excuses, perhaps predominant mannerisms that alert you to a simmering deception. Some kids look down; others get wide-eyed. Some shuffle around a bit; others stand pat and stare you down. The antidote, almost always, is to trust your instinct and slow the action down. Whether you are a parent, teacher, counselor, or member of the clergy, don't let a teen steamroll you with fast talk or dazzle you with details. If the facts don't make sense, demand more information, and let a kid know you're not so "out of it" or uncaring to let it slide. This tells them, in actions much louder than words, that you care about who they really are.

Adults with open eyes create traction; those whose eyes are shut unwittingly let kids slip away.

Securing the Empathic Envelope

The bottom line is not that children lie (you already know that), but that most no longer feel guilty or conflicted about it. Whatever style they use, they'll probably be good at it. This doesn't make our young people bad kids. But you need to be realistic. Kids will balk and scream, "You don't trust me." Of course (and this remains as true today as in previous generations) they will not be grateful until many years later. But you may see a surprising change in their behavior because, in essence, by stopping them, refusing to let teenagers spin out of control and take you for a fool, you are strengthening the empathic envelope—and lessening the dangers of the second family.

A story Myra, thirteen-year-old Jessica's mother, told me illustrates this point. Myra overheard Jessica's end of a phone conversation and gathered that her daughter was helping plan an unsupervised keg party. (This is a growing phenomenon throughout the country: several kids locate a house where parents are out of town, make all the arrangements, and charge their thirteen- to eighteen-year-old friends an admission fee to get in.) Myra was shocked at what she thought she was hearing, so she checked out the story with Jessie, who not only lied but went ballistic at her mother's intrusiveness.

"How dare you listen in when I'm on the phone! Who the hell do you think you are?" she shouted.

Myra wisely ignored the charge, refusing to back down. "Well? Are you planning this party or not?"

Within minutes, Myra managed to get enough of the story out of Jessica to say, "Forget it. They're going to have to have this party without you, because your father and I absolutely forbid you to go."

"You *have* to let me go," countered Jessica. "No one else is stopping their kid from going." Another lie: In truth, *none of the other parents knew.*

Myra didn't buy it. "Absolutely not. End of discussion. You're not going." This mom stuck to her guns, refusing to allow Jessica's lying, ranting, or pouting to sway her. Minutes later, she overheard another conversation.

"I can't go," Jessica mumbled into the phone. "My mom busted me. You're going to have to count me out."

Now here's the amazing part. Later that evening, Jessica came downstairs and sidled up to Myra, who was reading a book. She put her head on Myra's shoulder, apparently no longer angry. "Caroline's not going either. Neither is Hannah." As it turned out, one by one, Jessie's girlfriends also came up with an excuse not to attend the party.

"Mom?" Jessica then asked, as if nothing had happened.

"What, Hon?"

"Let's say I did go to that party or some other party. What if a boy I don't like wants to kiss me or asks me to take my top off?"

Jessica and Myra's story underscores the fact that kids, younger adolescents especially, may not *want* their parents to rein them in when they begin to stray but they *need* it. It's no accident that a recent TV commercial for a beeper company dramatizes this same phenomenon. A teenage boy and girl are alone on the porch of the house. Just as the boy is about to kiss his date, her beeper goes off. "Uh-oh," she says quickly, "Sorry. I have to go home." Cut to her house where her mother is waiting in the living room. "Thanks, Mom," the girl says as she bounds through the front door, obviously relieved.

The point is, kids *need* to be held by their parents and other adults in their life (more about this in Chapter 8). Too much distance is upsetting and scary. Drifting further and further into the second family, with no gravitational pull from their first family or from other concerned adults, invariably leads to dangerous behavior. All children need adults to strengthen the empathic envelope; it makes them feel safe and protected. Admittedly, this is hard to do in everyday life, especially where teenagers are concerned. One minute, adolescents want to move into their own apartment, the next, they're cuddling on a parent's lap. As an articulate thirteen-year-old said to me, "I want my freedom, but I don't really want to be on my own."

"I Don't Get It"

When we reinforce the empathic envelope, we let teens see we're not stupid and certainly not worthy of contempt. But there's another reason to be vigilant, to say no to unsupervised parties, and to refuse to back down when kids make bad decisions. Most teenagers are simply not going to make better choices on their own: *they don't understand why they should; they don't perceive inherent dangers; they don't understand adult rationale.*

The truth, which many adults find hard to believe, is that teens are less sophisticated than we think. Despite the fact that children nowadays are often so verbally adept, *they often don't know right from wrong or even why we demand the things we do.* How could this be? After all, so many kids are like budding attorneys; others spin miraculously embellished stories, or think several moves ahead. They all seem so precocious, it's hard to imagine that under the subterfuge, there's real confusion.

The proof is in scenes such as this, which happen every day in homes throughout America: As Georgina, mother of fifteen-year-old Joanna, walks by her daughter's bedroom and notices the TV on, she says (for the umpteenth time), "Have you finished your homework?"

"Stop bothering me about my homework," Joanna bellows. "I'm taking care of it. It's *my* homework, and it's *my* life." Georgina drops the subject (for now), but she is worried. Joanna is already on academic probation, the result of a year's worth of missed assignments, tardiness, and failed tests. (Mom doesn't realize yet that this is just the tip of the iceberg: her daughter's second-family crowd is also into shoplifting and drinking and Joanna has already slept with several boys and a couple of girls.)

An hour goes by, and still not a book is cracked open.

"If I had said another word about it at that point," sighs a defensive Georgina when she reports this story, "there would have been an even greater explosion. She'd probably tell me I'm trying to control her, like she always does. And she *still* wouldn't have done her homework."

Sounds familiar, I'm sure. Exasperating, no doubt. How often has your teenager gotten into trouble and blamed *you* for it? Or, you ask your surly adolescent to clean his room, set the table, help out with a younger sibling, or pick up a coat he dropped at the front door—and get this prepackaged response: "*Why* do I have to?" You think such tactics are always evasive ploys. But, the surprising truth is, whether it's about daily issues or more dangerous activities, *teenagers don't get it.* They often don't understand why we ask certain things of them or why we do what we do to protect and teach them.

On one hand, the culprit is developmental—generally, until around age sixteen, most children lack the neurological apparatus to handle abstract thinking. Thus, when you sit your kid down and demand to know *why* she did something, you're met with a vacant stare or a mumbled, "I dunno."

Another reason astonishingly glib thirteen-going-on-thirty adolescents are more *un*aware than most adults could possibly imagine is that the second family is like a business. And kids—its customers—are always right. Teenagers are accustomed to regulating their own pleasures, and when something or someone threatens their comfort, they feel wronged.

Remember Austin's reaction when her parents picked her up at the police station? There was no "I'm sorry I disappointed you, Mom and Dad," no hint of "Please don't be angry at me"—just her indignance. Austin simply couldn't grasp the notion that the neighbors and police had every reason to intercede when some fifty out-of-control teenagers were ransacking a house, getting drunk and stoned, and possibly committing grand theft. This wasn't just a matter of her being a good lawyer. *She didn't understand.*

As outrageous as this sounds, Austin is quite typical. I hear similar complaints from other kids who are caught, grounded, or in some way stripped of privileges because of their own wrongdoing. And for a long time, I, like their parents and teachers, kept trying to help these kids understand what they'd done. But the more I tried, erroneously assuming that they *could* understand, the more I pushed them away.

Eventually, I realized that to many teens, facts and truth are irrelevant abstractions that can't easily be grasped. Somehow incidents like the raid on Austin's keg party get turned around in kids' minds. It all seems so black-and-white to adults, yet teens, especially younger adolescents, experience themselves as the persecuted ones. From where they sit, their parents, teachers, and guidance counselors are wrong, or at the very least, grossly unfair. It's hard to fathom that in so many instances, seemingly articulate, modern kids simply "don't get" their impact, or understand why their behavior could be wrong. But it's true. In fact, often, when an adult is disappointed, hurt, inconvenienced, or injured by something a youngster does, in a teenager's head, it's the adult's own fault for not seeing it coming.

That's how Van justified the prank phone calls he had been making to a well-known national charity organization. "She's just sitting there asking for it," he said, referring to the poor, beleaguered receptionist who had fielded his calls for more than a week. I was shocked. Did he even consider the woman's feelings? Could he imagine why it wasn't a nice thing to do? Did it dawn on him that he was tying up the line, preventing serious callers from getting through? Over and over, I heard the same flat "no" from Van. He just didn't get it.

Granted, some kids will hazard a guess when forced to explain their behavior. When I asked Madison if she knew it was wrong to call a classmate "a worthless skank," she quickly answered, "yes." But when I then pressed and asked *why*, this otherwise smart kid stared blankly and said, "I don't know."

When Mitchell failed to do his term paper, I asked, "Don't you realize you're going to get an incomplete and that's not going to look good on your high school record?"

"No, not really," he answered, patently bored with our conversation. "I don't know why we have to do this stuff. It won't matter in my life."

And there's Steven, our ace plotter, who managed to get across the country without his parents even realizing that he had left town. His scheme was exposed when a desert windstorm bollixed his return flight. To this day, though, Steven still doesn't think he did anything wrong. The problem was simply that he got caught. In fact, he continues to insist that he could have gotten away with it . . . if it hadn't been for the storm.

I've learned in my own practice (and, I dare say, with my own kids), that if I hope to make any sort of connection, I have to gauge each child's limit of understanding. With adolescents, then, I start with the assumption that, no matter how savvy, well-spoken, and acutely perceptive in other areas of life kids might be, they really may not grasp what they did wrong or why all the grownups around them are so upset. The area of conflict doesn't matter. All the sermons under the sun won't make that teenager understand what you're talking about. It could be sloppiness, school performance, smoking, or sexual indiscretions. The more we adults accept this axiom—that many kids simply don't get it— the better our chances of finding other ways to get through to children and, ultimately, to connect.

You might be a bit confused at this point. After all, didn't I stress earlier that these kids are so much more psychologically aware than we were at this age and that they speak the language of therapy? Just as most adults are better at seeing others' than they are at seeing their own behavior, today's teenagers are similarly, and sometimes shockingly, unreflective about *themselves*. At the same time, though, they *are* often quite accurate about adults' vulnerabilities. Students of the media, they have learned about emotions and psychological motivation, and they can apply this learning to other people. From TV dramas and soap operas and talk shows, they've learned what being "depressed" or being "controlling" looks like. They can recognize when someone is a "workaholic" or an "addict"—words that simply weren't part of teen vocabulary in the past.

The paradox, then, is that although adolescents may not be able to see themselves, or understand their own motives, they can often see us more clearly than we see ourselves. Our job, then, is to not only listen to what our teenagers have to say, but to understand what we need to *do* differently to get through. The next chapter discusses why changing our steps in dances with kids is such a tough assignment, not just for parents, but for all adults.

6

"Listen to Me!"

Increasing Empathy and Self-Reflection

Adults and teens often find themselves caught in a "dance"—fruitless exchanges that lead to the same old arguments and cause kids to tune out. Changing the dance enables us to see both our children and ourselves more clearly. To do that, though, we have to learn how to listen instead of automatically losing it. Unfortunately, adolescents usually talk when it's hardest for adults to hear.

Caught in a Dance

When Aaron's parents separated, Kathleen, his mother, who had always been the more protective parent anyway, increased her vigilance. A high school sophomore when his parents' messy divorce was finalized, Aaron opted to spend more and more time at his dad's house. Wanting to escape his mother's watchful eye, he cut short visits at Mom's apartment, dodged her phone calls, and always had a good excuse for not being available—homework, after-school activities, plans with friends. Eventually, that wasn't enough. Aaron wanted to get away altogether, so he convinced his parents that he'd do better in boarding school. By his senior year, mother and son found their way into my office because even though Aaron's boarding school performance was fine, he'd almost completely shut down toward Kathleen.

First, Mom let fly a litany of complaints. "You're disrespectful. You're surly. When you talk to me, you're dismissive and you *never* listen to anything I tell you. What's wrong with you?"

When it was finally his turn, Aaron let her have it: "What's wrong with *me?* Whenever I say *anything,"* he yelled at her, "you always go one step ahead and try to come up with a solution. Sometimes I'd like a chance to figure things out for myself."

I urged Aaron to give his mother a concrete example: "You call me at school and say, 'When are you coming home during break?' I tell you what my plans are. The next thing I know, *you've* set up dinner and a night together, without checking with me."

Aaron and Kathleen were caught in a "dance"—a fruitless and repetitive exchange that, I was fairly sure, typified their every interaction. We all find ourselves in this position. We might say to ourselves, "If I only had a tape of this argument, I could play it every time the subject comes up." That's when you know you're doing the same old dance—and it's one of the main reasons we have trouble getting through to our kids (or, for that matter, to anyone else in our lives with whom communication breaks down).

Parents and other adults in positions of authority often become stuck in a particular dance when they deal with children. They find themselves saying the same things, making the same complaints or getting into arguments that always center on the same problem. Often, parents and teenagers have been doing a particular dance for years—a series of the same actions and reactions. The details change, but the quality of the interaction never does. It's an almost unavoidable fact of parenting. However, when any grownup—it could be a teacher, not just a parent—gets stuck in a particular dance, the child eventually tunes out the adult and vice versa.

Recognizing the Dance

Fortunately, during the session with Aaron, a light went on in Kathleen's eyes. She heard the kernel of truth in Aaron's angry outburst: she *did* have a tendency to rush in and fix whatever she thought needed fixing. She even admitted to Aaron, who thought he was her only "project," that some of her friends complained about the same thing. Her willingness to be accountable instantly diffused the tension. From then on, though, Kathleen had to practice holding back.

"I've gotten a little better," she reported months later. "I try to take a few deep breaths when Aaron confides in me. Instead of blurting out what I think he should do, I just think about what I normally would say—and then I try my best *not* to say it. I'm not always successful, but our relationship is changing, so I must be doing it at least some of the time."

Kathleen and Aaron's relationship is improving because she has increased her empathy for her son. She is better able to listen, without judging him. She has also improved her own capacity for self-reflection.

It's not easy for adults to see themselves; it's painful to look at one's own vulnerabilities head on. Still, when one is caught in a dance with an adolescent, it's a sure sign that somehow the balance between empathy and expectation has tipped—at worst, to one extreme or the other. But adults need to provide *both*, especially when it comes to teenagers. Empathy doesn't work without expectations and vice versa. If there is empathy without expectation, as when permissive parents or teachers lean more toward understanding, teenagers may feel "heard," but they don't feel held. If there is expectation without empathy, as when authoritarian adults stress rules and consequences, teenagers may toe the line or, worse, up the ante—get into even more trouble. Either way, *they don't feel known*. However, when adults achieve a balance, responding to the everyday moments in teenagers' lives in a way that demonstrates both authority *and* compassion, teenagers feel understood and more open to guidance.

In order to change the dance you have to be aware of it. That's the tricky part. Sadly, some adults are better than others at seeing not just the dance, but how their part perpetuates it. If you listen carefully, and without judgment, adolescents tell you all you need to know about the dance. Unfortunately, this usually happens at the most trying times.

Listening When You're Likely to Lose It

Teens talk when adults find it hardest to listen: when they want something from you or when they're in trouble. Understandably, these are the very moments when you, being exasperated, angry, or fearful, if not

all three, are most likely to lose it. At those times—when children negotiate, threaten, cry, defy, yell, stamp their feet, or storm out of the
room—what's actually happening is that they're pushing the edges of
the envelope. On the one hand, they're trying to expand its boundaries;
on the other, they need it to remain intact.

Adolescents have always pushed parents' limits, and I might add,
teachers', to the max. But given the potential dangers kids nowadays
seem to court, the stakes are higher. In the face of disrespect, the relentless negotiating, outright defiance, lies, and the outlandish behavior
so many teens exhibit, it makes sense that rather than listen and be
compassionate about *their* side of a story, we'd want to, quite simply,
ground them for life. When children throw caution to the wind, even
permissive parents want to reel them in. Who wouldn't understand why
Keith's mother would be distraught about her son's plans to sleep on
the beach in the dead of winter (see page 106)? Who wouldn't shudder
thinking about what will (not what could) be going on at that beach?
Would we be surprised if she not only denied his request but angrily
locked him in his room?

Likewise, when Jan, a respected high school teacher, moved with her
three adolescent sons to a more upscale neighborhood, she specifically
appealed to them: "Now that we're living here, the one thing I *don't*
want you to do is to publicly embarrass us." Within a matter of days,
the boys ended up at the local police station, pulled in for trespassing
and vandalizing. Who would blame Jan for feeling humiliated by her
sons' shenanigans, for going berserk when the police called? Nor would
it be surprising if she had trouble listening to her sons' explanations.

This is not to say that adults should forgo consequences in favor of
compassion. But you will find that your teen is *most open* during, and
especially after, those frightening arguments and unexpected crises that
have become ordinary occurrences, times when they've gone out and
created your worst nightmare—in essence, done exactly what you've
asked them *not* to do. Not surprisingly, those are the most difficult times
for a parent or an adult on the front line—in a classroom, running a
teen group, or a sports activity—to be empathic. But experience suggests
that this is precisely when it's most important to remain calm, open,

and nonjudgmental. Later, there will be time for punishment and laying down rules.

Emotionally, how do you manage that kind of restraint? Just as you're becoming most agitated, ready to tear your hair out—you need to stop and take a deep breath. Know that you'd *like* to explode, that you have every right to, and that later you can mete out the appropriate discipline. But, for the moment, you must seize this rare opportunity to *change the dance*.

Keep in mind, too, that the goal of many interactions with a teenager is to connect, to increase your knowledge and understanding of that child, so that guidance becomes possible. Remember that adolescence *per se* doesn't stop communication—teens *are* willing to talk—it's the fact that adults often can't muster the empathy that's needed to really listen. It doesn't matter if the infraction is talking back, cutting school, or getting arrested, whether teens lie about relatively benign situations or manufacture huge whoppers involving other kids and intricate schemes, this axiom always applies. When bad things happen, big or small, that's when teens open up—and a wise adult takes a beat and really listens.

A consummate example of this occurred a few years ago with Wendy, a mother whose fifteen-year-old son Peter took LSD and came home in the middle of a panic attack. A child of the '60s herself, Wendy had watched a good friend have an emotional breakdown after taking acid. She had always been forthright about her own fears and, for years, Peter had steadfastly promised her that he wouldn't experiment with drugs. Wendy believed him.

Like most parents and children, Wendy and Peter had a "dance." Wendy, a chronic worrier, saw danger around every corner. To protect him, she had set many rules and requirements but didn't have quite as much empathy for her son's changing needs as he moved into adolescence. This common imbalance in the empathy/expectation equation prevents adults from seeing who kids really are. Wendy, so busy lecturing and laying down the law, didn't catch the inconsistencies in Peter's stories or realize that he had been a "player"—sleeping around and smoking pot, for a good two years before he finally tried acid.

"There he was, tripping his brains out—my worst nightmare," said Wendy, recalling the wild look of panic in Peter's eyes, his rumpled clothing, the mysterious bruise on his forehead. "But I knew that right then and there, I had to make a choice. Was I going to lecture him and be angry, because he had done just the opposite of what I had asked and what he had promised? Or, was I going to listen and take care of him? Somehow I knew which was the right choice. I swallowed hard and put away all my rage. I just sat by him and talked softly, telling him it was going to be all right. Then I began to really listen."

Jan also took the high road when she collected her sons at the police station. "I had to get past my own disappointment and figure out what could possibly have possessed them to act out so blatantly." Instead of taking it personally, which admittedly would have been most parents' response, Jan, like Wendy, listened. "As it turned out, her sons had their own concerns about not being accepted in the new neighborhood." Finally, given an opportunity to express himself, her older son told her he was worried because they didn't have as much money as the other kids—how could they keep up? The younger boy missed his old chums, and he was sure that he wouldn't find new friends here.

I've seen teachers exercise the same restraint during the most difficult moments. Mrs. Hendricks, a guidance counselor who had been talking to the ninth-graders about the dangers of infection from piercing and tattooing, shuddered as she listened to fourteen-year-old Hillary boast about piercing her own nipple. She later admitted how hard it was not to be outraged, but to just sit there and listen. But she also knew that if she had any hopes of connecting with Hillary, she had to lead with empathy.

In these situations and others in which I've seen grownups set their relationships with teenagers on a better course, the adults had to push past their own hopelessness and disbelief about what the child had done. Then they dug deep down inside themselves in order to react empathically and to listen without harsh judgment. Discipline came later.

Listening for Our Part: Teens See What We Don't

Listening not only changes the dance, it also gives adults important information about themselves. Indeed, in the midst of a "scene," when a child is angry, scared, defensive, or in serious trouble, grownups hear what *they* need to do differently. Following are several examples of pivotal moments when adults finally heard something *about themselves* that enabled them to restore a balance between empathy and expectation. In some of these situations, grownups started out having high expectations but little empathy; in others, they had far more empathy for a child than expectations. In either case, though, the adults saw *their own part*. They were able to stop, pay attention to what the teen was saying, and recognize that there was an important truth to be learned: they realized that only by changing their own behavior could they change the nonproductive dance.

Wendy: Overprotective

Wendy heard a kernel of truth in Peter's acid-induced ranting, which included this invective: "You can't keep me in a bubble!" She *had* been overprotective, and rather than become fearful like his mother, Peter set out to prove to himself that he could handle anything. Wendy realized she had to tone down her constant fear-mongering.

Years later, Peter told me that his mother's ability to listen and not judge him in that nightmare of a moment permanently changed their relationship for the better. "I really got that she cared about *me*, not about being right or proving that she was the boss." Though Peter didn't articulate this in so many words, what really happened was that by listening, Wendy realized she had to act differently—she changed the dance—which, in turn, forced Peter to do different steps as well. She also grounded Peter; it took him months to earn back his freedom. But the punishment would have been far less effective—perhaps counterproductive—had she not first connected with Peter on an emotional level. Not so coincidentally, in the months that followed, Peter began to study more diligently with one of the better students in his second family.

Jan: A Steamroller

When Jan was at the police station with her sons, the older boy yelled at her, "You always force us to do things." At that moment, Jan recognized that she probably *had* been a bit of a steamroller around the recent move, owing to her own anxieties. Part of Jan's dance was to reframe difficult situations in the most positive light—teachers, after all, love constructive action. When she was preparing her sons for the move, Jan talked about only its best aspects, without acknowledging the enormity of change and the potential challenges it would bring. Moreover, she was a powerful woman accustomed to training and directing people. At home, she routinely issued edicts to her sons. Unable to confront her strong personality in a more direct manner (a problem some of her subordinates had as well), the boys continuously defied Jan behind her back. That was their dance.

Now, in the face of this more blatant act, as Jan listened to her older son's charge, she was able to slow down, " 'fess up," and apologize for not taking their feelings into account. Finally, Mom stopped being the teacher and, despite her immediate desire to come down hard on the boys, she first listened to them. In other words, she changed the dance. That is not to say that she didn't ground them for their trouble with the police; they had to take responsibility for *their* part, too. But because she approached the situation with more openness and self-appraisal, because she was able to be understanding *as well as* authoritative, she earned their respect. This balance between empathy and expectations strengthened the first-family envelope. The boys not only became more cooperative at home, in their second family they now gravitated toward a less-troubled group of kids.

Mona and Jack: Talking without Listening

With Frank, the "liar" you first met in Chapter 3 (page 63), after months of therapy and threats, he finally seemed to be doing his homework more regularly, handing in term papers, and, in general, functioning a little better in school. But just as his parents, Mona and Jack, who co-owned a successful neighborhood business, thought he was out of the woods, Frank defiantly smoked up on school campus at the end of his junior year. All the grownups were understandably devastated. In my office, and on the phone with me, they took him to task, bombarding him with questions, demanding explanations:

"How could you do this?"

"What were you thinking?"

"Didn't you know you'd get caught?"

"How will you ever get into college?"

"What are you going to make of yourself?"

"Don't you think everyone's given you enough chances?"

Frank was mute during a ten-minute harangue in my office. Like all the adults around, his parents were asking questions Frank couldn't answer. When Mona and Jack finally wound down, they looked in my direction, hopelessly. I nodded at Frank, indicating that it was his turn. I wasn't all that hopeful myself, assuming he'd do what he usually did: give us the silent treatment. To my surprise, once they stopped their typical response and seemed willing to listen rather than just lash out at him, Frank let loose with a tirade of his own:

"Why don't you two ever leave me alone? I've told you a thousand times . . . you're always grilling me. Why *should* I tell you what's going on? You don't listen anyway. When I answer, you twist what I say to make it sound like what *you* want to hear. Stop telling me what I think and what I'm like. You don't have a clue—you *all* don't have a clue. *This* is why I'd rather hang out with my friends. They don't ask me anything. You think I'm just like you—big, important, in charge. Well, I'm not. You don't care about *my* feelings. All you care about is looking good in front of other people."

What a mouthful! With my encouragement, Mom and Dad changed the dance: they simply held their tongues. In turn, Frank began to talk. He could see that even though he may have said the same thing to his parents "a thousand times," for once they were actually listening.

Granted, Frank was being defensive (and offensive). What he had done was wrong and he needed to experience real consequences. But there also was more than a smattering of truth in what he had to say. Mona and Jack *were* enormously powerful people; so were his dean and school counselor. They all *did* grill him constantly with unanswerable questions and Frank would just sit there. Their dance was always the same: the parents' verbal barrage, the professionals' endless questions, were met by the boy's silence. But at that moment, in the face of such a huge disappointment over Frank's blatant disregard for school rules, and despite the desire to wring his neck or at least elicit answers from him, both parents did something different: they stopped, changed the dance, and allowed Frank to express himself. In doing so, Frank gave Mona and Jack (and the other adults involved) a clue about how to get to him: stop grilling. To their credit, they took heed.

Felicia and Seymour: Lacking Teamwork

Felicia and Seymour were at the other end of the continuum—they had lots of empathy for their children but expected very little. Fourteen-year-old Todd, their older child, was on the verge of being expelled. Felicia, who believed that it was important to give a child respect, was endlessly patient with him when he missed homework assignments or came home with bad grades, or stayed out past curfew with a girl. Besides, Todd always had a good excuse. Her frustration only leaked out when she fought with her son about his room being so messy or his refusal to help clean up after dinner. Most arguments ended with his slamming doors and her throwing up her hands in defeat. Seymour wasn't much help. He had decided early on in Todd's life that schoolwork and chores were "Felicia's department," so he rarely got involved.

On one particular evening, though, when Felicia unconvincingly threatened to dock Todd's allowance if he didn't become "more responsible," her son upped the ante. He picked up his baseball bat and swung it wildly in Mom's direction. Then he ranted, in a way that only a modern kid would dare do, "Responsible? You want me to be more responsible, but you're such a wimp, and Dad's such an asshole!"

The kernel of truth in those words, even more than the baseball bat her son was wielding, stopped Felicia in her tracks. She recognized that she *was* always apologizing and running interference so as not to disturb Seymour with the insignificant details of childrearing. In doing that, she realized, she had inadvertently prevented Todd from knowing his dad and vice versa. To Felicia's surprise, Seymour suddenly jumped in and pried the bat from Todd's hands. He heard something, too, for it was the first time he'd gotten so directly involved in one of the frequent outbursts between his wife and son.

Naturally, the family had to get immediate counseling and there were serious consequences for Todd's behavior. However, the incident created a dance-stopping opening. In shock and terrible fear, Mom and Dad interrupted the usual steps and listened as Todd complained to his father, "When you're at home, Dad, you only work. You've been doing that since I was a little kid, and nothing gets you to change. I need it to be different, and so does my sister." Todd then admitted, "I'm not really mad at Mom — it's just that she's the one who's usually here. You've never been around."

Seymour understood; his son's words rang true. With tears in his eyes, he recounted his own father's absence. It was the beginning of a major shift in this family — Dad started to get home a little earlier and actually pay attention to some of Todd's interests. Quietly, over time, these two disconnected family members began to know each other. Both parents also started to put more limits on Todd's comings and goings. Felicia let him know that she *expected* him to do his chores and his schoolwork, and there would be consequences if he didn't comply. By working as a team for the first time ever, these parents made their son earn his privileges. It was no coincidence that Todd's almost invisible slide toward the second family slowed down and his performance in school improved.

Margaret: Being a Doormat

Margaret, the mother of fourteen-year-old Lauren, discovered a shocking scene — her daughter having sex in the bathtub with two boys at the same time. Up to that point, it had been a rocky year in which Lauren had been spinning out of control. She had dyed her hair orange and blue, gotten a tattoo, even pierced her tongue and eyebrow, and with each increasingly extreme act, Margaret had tried her best to be "reasonable." She asked Lauren why. She bared her own soul about what it was like to grow up in the '60s, with a very repressive mother who questioned her every move. She didn't want to be that way with Lauren.

Margaret, who had endless empathy but asked little in return, kept hoping that her unceasing understanding would encourage Lauren to mend her ways. Instead, her daughter's behavior became even more outrageous, culminating in the bathtub incident.

"I wasn't doing anything," Lauren protested, even after Margaret threw the boys out of the house. "You must have been imagining it, because *your* mother was so strict and you were wild as a kid. Now you think that's what I'm doing. Besides, there were bubbles in the tub—how could you know what was actually going on?"

Margaret stopped and, for a brief moment, doubted herself. She almost went back to being the understanding Earth Mother. But then she became incensed. "What do you think I am—a damn fool?"

"Yes," said Lauren, deadpan.

Suddenly, Margaret heard the truth: she *had* been a fool. She had allowed Lauren to talk her out of one limit after another. She had been a virtual doormat. Having heard the truth and faced it, Margaret did what any responsible parent would do: she grounded Lauren until she trusted her enough to go out again (more about making teenagers *earn* privileges in the next chapter). She continued to have compassion, but now it was counterbalanced with consequences. Not surprisingly, her daughter began to talk about what was going on inside her emotionally. As it turned out, she had been hiding an eating disorder and an obsessive preoccupation with her body. Sex was the only thing, Lauren finally admitted, that made her feel in control and confident.

■

In each of the preceding cases, it's clear, the dance only stops when adults are willing to listen and, just as important, to be accountable *for their own behavior*. Granted, it's hard to hear from a child that you're unreasonable, self-absorbed, controlling, or any of the other allegations I've heard teenagers hurl at parents, teachers, counselors—even clergy. However, listening and being accountable is the best way I know for any adult to correct the imbalance. Where parents leaned too far to the rigid side, they saw that they needed to become more understanding. Where there was too much empathy, they began reining an adolescent in with enforceable, realistic limits. In each situation, the balance strengthened the envelope: the first family became a stronger force in the child's life, if not stronger than the second family, at least equal to it. Kids experienced more comfort at home, because they felt *known*. In turn, the more dangerous, disconnected, and frighteningly dangerous aspects of the pop culture and peer network lost some of their allure.

When the Envelope Breaks

Sadly, I've seen a fair share of cases in which adults refuse to see their own role in what's going on. The impasse is never resolved for one if not both of these reasons: the grownup feels so humiliated by the child's actions, so publicly embarrassed, that he or she is afraid to let go even a little bit, for fear that the situation could become even worse; or he or she believes the problem is solely located within the child. In such cases, the second family retains its prominence, for it is the one place where the child is known and can find comfort, understanding, and clear expectations.

I saw this kind of impasse between Brenda and her mother, Arlene. Brenda, a sophomore in high school, was drifting toward the second family, and Arlene's primary strategy was to lecture. Brenda described their dance perfectly: "She gets so hysterical. Everything I say makes her nervous—whatever I wear, let's say a cool hat or goth stockings, stresses her out. I can't get her to back off. She just keeps talking and explaining and convincing me to do what she thinks is right."

In a joint session with mother and daughter, I tried to get Arlene to see that the sermons and rebukes were just increasing the distance between Brenda and her. "This is how I am," said Arlene definitively. "I can't be different. I don't want to be."

Sadly, Arlene remained true to her word, and Brenda drifted farther and farther from her. By her junior year, she secretly got involved with drugs and was sexually active with partners she met in chat rooms. One such encounter, in which Brenda had agreed to meet a man in a multileveled parking lot, almost led to rape. Thankfully she talked her way out of being harmed. Not sufficiently scared, Brenda's acting up became more public. She began to wear micromini skirts and low-cut sweaters to school, outfits so provocative she was sent home several times. With grades falling, Brenda was finally asked to leave school. Clearly, Brenda's troubles were not simply her mother's *fault*. However, had Arlene been able to change the dance—listen as well as lecture and set limits— perhaps some progress could have been made that might have prevented her daughter from slipping so far away.

The same unfortunate breach happens in schools, where there also needs to be a balance between empathy and expectations. (Actually, the empathic envelope should *include* the school, not just a child's family; more about this in Chapter 8.) For example, the teachers who came in contact with Jordan, a young adolescent headed down the road to academic failure, had great difficulty seeing that there were kernels of truth in Jordan's allegation, "They don't really care about what I do or what I am." From my perspective, Jordan had a point, and his teachers' actions spoke louder than their protestations.

"He's making his own bed. These are his choices," said the guidance counselor when Jordan had repeatedly failed to show up for class.

"He's got to suffer the consequences when he hands papers in late," said his social science teacher. Jordan had missed one deadline after another in the man's class.

The counselor and several of Jordan's teachers clung to that philosophy for many months. Of course, they were partially correct: adolescents have to understand cause-and-effect, that adults have expectations. But Jordan also needed to be heard. That's the empathy side of the equation.

As long as this stalemate continued, Jordan's behavior continued to escalate. He was partying every weekend, doing more exotic drugs, like Ecstasy and hashish, hooking up with as many girls as possible. There is no doubt that this boy was already in serious danger. As long as his teachers refused to budge from their hard-nosed position and, in addition to punishing him, take a look at who he really was, Jordan was headed for disaster.

Restoring the Balance

I finally convinced the administration and teachers to agree to a trial period, during which they'd demonstrate to Jordan that there were limits *and* that they also cared. When he was absent, someone called the house to find out why. When he complained, they listened, instead of summarily judging him and assuming he was about to utter the same old excuses. In other words, I got them to stop thinking in such a linear fashion, which didn't mean abandoning the notion that Jordan needed rules. It meant also finding out more about him—what he was interested in, his likes and dislikes. They also started talking to him *with* his friends, so they began to see that the Jordan they knew was different with his second family. Eventually, word got out that Jordan was a computer genius, and instead of seeing him as an adversary, school personnel began to see him as an asset. The guidance counselor, who was writing a book, asked his advice on what kind of word-processing program to buy. The principal asked for his help in setting up the school's Web site. In essence, the adults were able to shift out of the unbalanced mode. Jordan is still not even close to being an avid student. But more of his work is now being done on time. He still lies occasionally but not as flagrantly as he used to. Just as important, though, his relationships in the first family at home were also salvaged. Mutual respect is now part of everyday life—the adults whom he once fled are slowly becoming as real to him as the lures of the second family.

■

As happened with Jordan, when grownups change the dance and then listen to the kernel of truth in a child's ranting, they are able to establish that all-important balance. The dance is interrupted, and, there is real possibility for connection. Only small changes happen at first, but then success builds on success. Adults don't instantly change and neither do adolescents.

Again, let me stress that parents and teachers still need to set limits. When kids aren't where they're supposed to be or don't do what is expected, a grownup has to respond, rein a child in. The parent or teacher listens, but they also don't allow themselves to be taken advantage of. Admittedly, in the everyday crunch of life, this is a fine line for anyone to walk. The next chapter, therefore, outlines concrete strategies that help adults slow down the action and get teenagers' attention.

7

"How Dare You!"

Dealing with Privacy, Confidentiality,
and Other Matters of Trust

Because today's adolescents feel entitled to independence, we need to motivate them to earn our trust, rather than assume that privileges and privacy are givens. Stepping in early, wrangling over privileges, and having clear expectations increase adult/teen contact and diminish the grip of the second family. Adults also must help teens balance schoolwork and fun in healthy ways, so second-family comforts are not as necessary to soothe overscheduled kids.

An Unbalanced World

In generations past, the adults' role in a community and in the family was to provide structure, rituals, and continuity. That's not happening now. The balance between empathy and expectations is seriously skewed. Kids are off in their own world. Today's adolescents can become masters of guilt-free deception. When they get into trouble, teens easily rattle off their "rights" and zealously barricade their personal "space."

Ian, caught red-handed with pot in his backpack (page 106), told his devastated mother, "If you hadn't been snooping, you wouldn't be so upset." The next day, acting the aggrieved party to the hilt (not unlike several other teens I've known), he installed a huge padlock and chain on his bedroom door.

I saw a similar reaction in thirteen-year-old Rose, who left her diary on the kitchen table. After seeing it there for several days, her mother, Jeanette, finally broke down and read the page that had been left open. To her shock, Jeanette learned that her daughter had been sneaking out of the house to have sex with her fifteen-year-old boyfriend *and* her best girlfriend.

"I don't care what you think!" Rose screamed when Jeanette confronted her. "It's your own fault for reading my diary. That's my private possession."

Kids' reactions tell us that the pendulum has swung way too far. It truly seems that the world has been torn down the center with kids living an alternate reality and adults wondering what to do.

"A day doesn't go by when I'm not shocked by something my seventh-graders say or do," remarks a teacher in a community workshop, describing twelve-year-old students selling Ritalin on campus. "I'm hearing and seeing things I used to associate only with older kids." Another teacher comments on being stunned when *seventh- and eighth-graders* come in on Monday, clearly trashed from binge-drinking, partying, and pot-smoking the previous weekend.

A mother in one of my workshops puts it more bluntly, shocking even the jaded parents sitting next to her: "My kids scare the shit out of me — and so do yours!" Why not? In this suburban community, the grownups had just discovered after-school parties with a new twist: hired strippers. This along with an alarming increase in their teens' use of heroin.

It's not that adolescents and even preteens don't particularly fear adult authority anymore (which most don't). They don't *need* parents, teachers, counselors, or clergy quite as much, because they have the second family to rely on. In too many cases, mother and fathers (and sometimes unsuspecting grandparents) are useful for money and a place to crash; teachers are but a passing blip on their often hazy, distracted daily consciousness. But as for connection and guidance, they turn to their buddies.

How, then, do adults create a safety net for kids? Anyone who deals with teenagers must accept this basic notion: privileges and privacy are not entitlements; they must be earned. As such, adults today *do* have something of great importance that kids must earn—*their trust*. However, my interviews with teens and with adults responsible for their welfare indicate that both generations assume just the opposite.

Parents: Keep Out!

Modern adolescents truly believe that privileges and privacy are inalienable rights and that adults have no business interfering in their lives. In teens' minds, expanding freedoms are rites of passage that accompany a particular birthday. This includes just about all privileges—going to the mall with friends, getting a learner's permit, going to a Friday-night movie straight from school, hanging out in chat rooms on the Internet, taking public transportation after dark, going to clubs and concerts, having sleepovers, even having sex. Just as Keith "informed" his mother that he and his buddies were going to sleep on the beach, teenagers everywhere *announce* their plans, rather than ask permission of parents and other adults.

Patrick, fifteen, tells his parents that Megan, his girlfriend from camp, will be visiting for the weekend. He informs them that Megan and he will sleep together in his room. When he repeats the story to me, I ask, "Are you allowed to just *demand* this of your parents?" He's stumped by the question; not one computer chip in his brain tells him he might be off-base.

Twelve-year-old Evie, assuming her parents wouldn't mind, casually mentions to Mom and Dad that six of her best friends would be sleeping over. She expects them not to question her, and they don't, not even when it turns out that her friends are a group of girls *and* boys. At one point, Mom walks by Evie's room and because the door happens to be open, peeks in. To her shock, Evie and her guests—fellow seventh-graders—are half-naked and giving each other massages.

The same attitudes of entitlement apply to privacy. Ever since the dawning of the self-esteem movement in the mid-'70s, children have begun to feel that privacy is another absolute right. Most kids believe that they have a right not to be spied on, and when any adult violates this conviction, they become enraged. A teenager's room is his or her sacred domain, never to be encroached upon by an adult. Some kids forbid Mom or Dad from entering even when they're not home.

Unfortunately, many parents foster these attitudes and unwittingly collude with kids' notions of freedom, which only strengthens their resolve. We don't expect to be asked. We are often skittish about entering our kids' rooms, guiltily calling it "snooping" when we do. Fearful of damaging a child's self-esteem, we worry that such intrusions are unhealthy. Consequently, teens feel justified in doing whatever they want in the sanctity of their own space. In adolescents' minds, parents simply cannot cross the line, even to save them. One mother barged in on her fifteen-year-old whom she suspected of cutting herself. The girl ended up in a psychiatric hospital, fuming at her mother. In all likelihood, Mom saved her daughter's life, but that didn't matter to the girl or her mother, who seriously questioned her actions, even though it was apparent that she had done the right thing.

Why are parents and other adults so doubtful of their own authority, so unsure of the expectation side of the equation? In part, it's because a majority of us are in the baby-boomer generation that actually ushered in the idea of children needing their own "space." In part, we are overreacting to our own childhood. Many grownups today were raised in enmeshed or chaotic families—and therefore know firsthand the dangers of allowing adults to cross boundaries and possibly violate a child. We patently state to all who care to listen, including our children, that we don't want to be like our own parents. We remember our hunger for freedom and privacy as teenagers and don't want to squelch children or make them feel "oppressed."

Moreover, thanks to favorable economics, many middle-class children have rooms, or at least their own area—a basement playroom, a crawl space—and we allow it to be theirs and theirs alone. Other than when a child blatantly leaves something in view—in which case, according to conventional wisdom, they are "asking" to be found out—it is somehow understood that enlightened adults respect kids and, therefore, choose not to invade their territory.

Again, the balance is askew: the emphasis is on parents earning kids' trust, instead of requiring *mutual* trust. When a child gives vague answers about her plans, puts a lock on her door, or even says, "Get out of my room," we consider such moments normal in today's world. So what if *our* parents would have never let us travel after dark, or go "clubbing"? Some of us even feel a bit of pride in the face of our children's assertiveness and independence. And because we don't want to appear old-fashioned, we accept that it's all quite reasonable.

But it isn't.

Evaluating What *Your* Child Needs

Privileges and privacy are *not* developmental—there are no strict age-related guidelines that tell us when it's right to grant a child more freedoms. These are *individual* matters that need to be negotiated on a child-by-child basis. When one girl turns fourteen, she may have the maturity to attend a rock concert without an adult, whereas another fourteen-year-old may not. When a boy, at sixteen, qualifies for a learner's permit, he may have the trustworthiness to become a driver, whereas another sixteen-year-old may not. And regardless of their exact age, just because teenagers hurl accusations of snooping at adults who check out backpacks, lockers, or dresser drawers, it doesn't mean that their space and property never warrant inspection.

Many kids, despite their seeming sophistication and glib remarks, often lack the inner resources to exercise caution and judgment. In a world where there is less supervision and complete access to dangerous exploits, adults simply cannot give in automatically, according to a developmental timetable. Grownups cannot allow teens to continue to move toward second-family activities without asking, "Is this child capable of handling this situation?" Even when children protest—and they will—too much latitude puts them at risk.

The critical task is to *know* a child and to gauge his or her readiness, and then to demand that the child *earn* your trust. The importance of this process was apparent in the very heartrending and nearly tragic case involving a recently divorced, suburban mom, Tina, and her teenage daughter, Rhea. At thirteen, Rhea was an underachiever, although obviously very bright. When her brother suddenly died in a camping accident, Rhea, who was already heading downhill, plunged even further. Her mother, Tina, understandably devastated about losing a child, was so happy to have her daughter alive, she put no constraints on her. Tina didn't realize that her trust was a valuable commodity; she just gave it freely to Rhea without making her daughter earn it.

Predictably, the more Rhea was left out there with her second family, the more she courted trouble. Tina realized the severity of the situation when she happened on Rhea's diary and discovered that her daughter had experimented with crack cocaine and multiple sex partners, exposing herself to addiction, pregnancy, STDs, and AIDS — in other words, risking everything. This vulnerable, caring mother felt like she had been punched in the stomach, realizing that in her grief and her desire to be understanding, she had inadvertently let her daughter slide into life-endangering situations.

With my help, Tina came down hard on Rhea, even though she had mixed feelings about imposing restrictions. This was a mother who needed no help in being empathic. She never wanted her daughter to feel repressed; as a result, she willingly and far too easily trusted her. Unless a situation was blatantly dangerous, she automatically allowed Rhea to participate. Now reading her daughter's diary, it was clear that Rhea had taken Tina's trust for granted and abused it. Fearing the prospect of losing yet another child — from behaviors she'd never imagined her daughter engaging in — Mom saw clearly that something had to be done. She needed to try a more a balanced approach with her child.

"I'm not going to let you continue to come and go without more supervision," she finally told her daughter, who immediately turned a cold shoulder — her mom's worst fear. Although it was clear that Rhea was starting to withdraw, Tina continued: "You're going to have to earn my trust from now own. No more carte blanche." Even as Rhea ranted about the invasion of her privacy, Tina explained her own fears. "I can't take a divorce and losing another child. I can't take worrying about you, not trusting you. I deserve to be treated better."

The day Tina was able to insist that her daughter *earn* her trust rather than allow her to take it for granted, as she had done, was the day that this young girl's life turned around. Rhea, realizing her mother could now listen without lecturing, slowly warmed up to Tina, opening up for the first time about her reaction to the divorce and the sudden death in their family. The two of them also went through their photo album and cried together over their devastating loss. This may sound like a miracle conversion, and in a way it was. Rhea started to do better in school and eventually stopped her casual sexual acting out, settling down with one boy. Rhea's attitude shifted as well; she became proud of being someone who kept her word.

The Unexpected Benefits of Conflict

It's no accident that through wrangling over the emotionally charged area of privacy, a mother got to know her daughter better and, in the process, strengthened the empathic envelope. Not surprisingly, the tenor of the household changed, too. Although Rhea probably couldn't have articulated it as such, on some level she felt that Tina was exhibiting *empathy* and having clear *expectations*. It changed everything about the way the two of them functioned.

Though the idea of negotiating with a teenager over privileges and privacy is daunting, it's important to remember that such interactions, heated or not, usually lead everyone to higher ground. Kids are most likely to open up when we engage them. These are the times when we learn who a child really is and can create a more realistic and personal empathic envelope to contain him or her. It's also a time when children are *motivated to open up*. If teens are in trouble, if they're afraid of losing precious rights, they're more willing to talk. In contrast, when adults back down from these talks, because they're frightened of confrontation or because there's not enough time, they unwittingly let opportunities to establish traction slip away.

For instance, after Ian blew up at his mother for snooping in his backpack and was similarly enraged at his father for having the temerity to keep him from going to an upcoming Dave Matthews concert, he promptly shut himself up in a closet—a teenage Gandhi on strike. His parents let him stew for a while and then his father, Simon, went into the closet to join him. Simon knew that because Ian so desperately wanted to go to the concert, his son would, at that moment, be motivated to open up.

Ian gave Simon the silent treatment at first, but as his dad began to talk about his own escapades as a boy, what he'd done wrong and what *his* father had done about it, Ian started to open up. In the first honest discussion this boy had had with his father in years, Ian talked about the drugs other kids were experimenting with and what it was like for him to make decisions about substances. Because Simon was being empathic, and because he listened to rather than judged his son, Ian began to talk about his own pot-smoking, too. Ian never got to see "Dave" — at least not *that* particular concert — but from then on, there was more of a balance between both parents' empathy and expectations.

In another home, Carl, who was just shy of thirteen, came home from school every day smelling of smoke. When his mother, Diane, a highly astute lawyer, asked his whereabouts, Carl, who was a member of the debating team, showed that he was every bit as good a litigator as she. For each outing, he concocted an airtight alibi. With a straight face, he would tell Diane he was going to Brad's house — but she shouldn't bother calling because they'd be watching a movie. If Mom did call to check, Brad would cover for him, saying that Carl had just left. Or, he would say he was going to hang out at the mall, and by the time she was ready to ask more questions, he'd be out the door. Although Diane had momentary misgivings, she nevertheless opted to believe her son. She didn't want to grill him; she wanted an open atmosphere; she wanted her son to trust *her*. Besides, Diane had faith in Carl, so it was hard for her to believe that he would be saying one thing and doing something completely different.

Months went by. One day, purely by chance, a neighbor spotted Carl at a nearby billiards parlor, where a group of older kids hung out, of course smoking, playing pool, and conning patrons (often, successfully) into buy them beer. When Diane later confronted him about what happened, Carl said indignantly, "Hey, I'm in eighth grade now. Don't you trust me? Anyway, it's my right to come and go as I please." After a series of explosive exchanges, he slammed the door to his room, and Diane called me.

"You've got to make him see that he's got it backward—he has to regain *your* trust. *Then* he'll be allowed privileges." I counseled her, in effect, to change the dance: "Tell him he has to earn his way back into the world."

Which is exactly what Diane did. She got him a beeper and, at first, put him on a very short leash. He had to check in every hour after school and tell her where he was going and offer some proof. So, if he was at Brad's house, he had to put Brad's mother on the phone (or another adult who was in charge). After initially balking, Carl, to her surprise, seemed almost relieved. He knew what was expected of him—he knew he had to earn Diane's trust and that she was going to hold him answerable. They had more talks. Diane learned a little more about who Carl was, the tough decisions he faced every day, which, in effect, closed the great gaping distance that had once existed between Carl's second family and his first.

Earning adult trust and being held accountable helps teenagers improve their judgment. Instead of allowing kids to do as they please, we open the envelope in small increments. Instead of accepting that privacy is an absolute right, never to be violated, we let them know that, as is the case with most privileges in life, one needs to *earn* rewards. Insisting that a teenager toe the line in this way—in other words, meet adult expectations—shores up the borders of the empathic envelope, creates the traction and connection that are a better match for the second family.

Remember fourteen-year-old Carter? He threw a party for three hundred of his closest friends when his parents went out of town attending to his dying grandmother (page 26). Given the endless number of beer cans strewn about, holes burned into the rugs, underwear and used condoms shoved under couches and beds, Mom and Dad, of course, wanted to ground him for the rest of his life. When they came to me, I pointed out that their parenting had leaned too much toward laissez-faire "empathy." As such, they had too freely given Carter their trust, believing his stories without checking them out. They had just assumed he'd be responsible, failing to take into consideration his maturity level and without Carter having a track record that actually demonstrated his reliability.

At my urging, Carter's mom and dad changed the dance by stripping him of all his privileges and then giving him a chance to earn back the rights he'd lost. They did this by instituting a system of responsibility and rewards—something they should have done in the first place. Things Carter had taken for granted, like using the telephone as much as he liked, they now restricted. Cutting off telephone contact with his friends for a month was like taking away his oxygen, but when they saw that he was abiding by their rules, they slowly began to grant permission—at first, just an hour's worth of phone calls a week. In time, they let him have one friend over after school—another "right" he formerly took for granted. The next step was to let him have an after-school date with a friend, but only if he proved that he could be home by five sharp. If, instead, he came home with some lame excuse for being late, he would go back to ground zero. Over a period of many months, he finally earned a Friday night out.

Throughout this period, earning their trust led to more talking—not entirely out of the goodness of his heart, but because Carter wanted and needed something from his parents. Instead of allowing him to take privileges for granted, his folks spent time talking about each new opening of the envelope. When adults make this effort to go over nitty-gritty details, the resulting interactions are more than a matter of laying down rules; they're a chance to really get to know that child. Parents and kids *touch* each other; kids rub up against adults, not just the second family.

Carter's parents still grounded him, still made him write letters of apology. But despite his flagrant infraction, they managed to listen and, thus, to get past their son's glib facade. As it turned out, members of his second family thought of him as a guy who always could be counted on. Because of his unerring evenhandedness, Carter was often the one who handled disagreements between friends. But few were there for *him*.

It's no coincidence that Carter didn't have any more parties after that. A balance between empathy and expectations had been reached. Carter didn't become a more responsible kid simply because he was afraid of the consequences of not living up to his parents' expectations, which would mean a further loss of privileges. Now he also *wanted* to prove his maturity to them, because he felt them so solidly in his corner, *and*, of course, he wanted his privileges back. Not so incidentally, he developed a relationship with a new kid in school who turned out to be a good listener and someone, now, whom *Carter* could depend on.

Sweating the Small Stuff

To be sure, adults *must* make children prove themselves *before* saying "yes," and yet anguished parents and teachers often find themselves deliberating these issues when it's too late. I hear laments such as these all the time:

"I shouldn't have let him go to the movies alone with his fourth-grade friends—I should have known they'd sneak into R-rated films."

"We shouldn't have left those kids unattended on the class trip. It's no surprise they shoplifted and acted so rudely to the storekeepers that they were thrown out."

"I smelled an odor coming from her room for the past few weeks. Instead of assuming that it was incense, I should have checked it out for myself."

"I shouldn't have let my fourteen-year-old attend that party without my knowing where the parents were—now he's got to struggle with herpes for the rest of his life."

"We should have searched his locker the very moment we thought he was bringing drugs into school."

Just as Monday-morning quarterbacks can't win yesterday's game, all the regrets in the world can't reverse the slide of a teenager in trouble. Therefore, rather than regret giving too much freedom or realize too late that you should have scrutinized more carefully teens' activities, *pay attention to small changes* and step in before something "big" happens. Let children know that you have specific expectations and, when those are not met, deal with little infractions before they turn into serious offenses.

This notion flies in the face of most of what we've read about teenagers. Parents, teachers, and guidance counselors are constantly reminded that they have to be on the lookout for so-called red flags—the danger signs of poor school performance, drug and alcohol use, sex, and other *big* issues. Adults are typically admonished to be clear about their standards. Tell children you don't want them to drink, smoke cigarettes, or indulge in illegal substances. Let them know that you expect them to do well in school, to be responsible about their bodies, to be thoughtful about sex.

There's nothing wrong with such advice, but from my experience and from the most recent research on teens, *it's the small details of kids' lives that not only tell us whether a teen is on the skids, but give adults ample opportunities to increase empathy and create realistic expectations.* In one study, conducted by the Johnston Institute in Minneapolis, which has been compiling patterns of substance abuse since 1990, it was documented that when parents consistently maintain expectations of children, their kids are less prone to risky behavior. In other words, be crystal clear about your standards and enforce them when even small problems crop up.

This may feel overwhelming to busy adults who often don't have the time or inclination to monitor every detail of a child's life. But in my experience, we need to *make* the time—and to view it as envelope maintenance. Whether it takes five minutes or a half hour, these hard discussions make a difference. When adults address what's happening in a kid's life, tell him or her what they expect, and then haggle over the specifics, they are most likely to connect. It's as if we hit the "pause" button for a second to break through the frenzied pace of daily life and can really get through to our children. And because kids want increased freedom or privileges from us, at those times they're more open to talking. If, on the other hand, we don't ask kids to *earn* our trust in this way, if we don't pay attention to the early clues they drop about themselves, youngsters have absolutely no need or motivation to discuss anything with an adult. They simply rush out, slip out, or fly out the door to the comfort of the second family.

Typically, minor lapses begin in grades six and seven. Studies tell us this in measurable ways. Children's self-care habits deteriorate. Teenagers in trouble eat worse, sleep less, bathe less, study less, care less about their clothing and their rooms. They have little interest in activities they once pursued with zeal, such as music lessons, sports, and hobbies; they care more about hanging out with their friends.

Unfortunately, these minor changes aren't usually on anyone's radar. Believing they had better watch out for *significant* academic problems, *dramatic* differences in sleeping and eating patterns, *sudden* loss or gain of weight, and other major diversions from the norm, most adults don't bother to think in terms of small expectations. They assume subtle changes are part and parcel of adolescence — evidence that their teen is "separating" from them and therefore inevitable. Besides, we're often told, "pick your battles." So what if a child is wearing the same clothes four days in a row? At least she's still doing okay in school. At least, she's not coming home more than ten or fifteen minutes after curfew.

Wrong.

In just about every case in which kids slip deeper into second-family trouble, their problems were preceded by breaches of small expectations, a subtle distancing that neither their parents nor other responsible adults heeded. For a long time, I didn't pay attention either, but reviewing many cases and workshop discussions showed me the danger of such ignorance.

At thirteen, Mark's grades started going down — not much, just a half grade. Where he once took at least one or two baths a week, his personal hygiene seemed to be declining. His appearance was more unkempt — like any other teenager with a new adolescent grunge image. Looking back, though, that was the beginning of Mark's immersing himself in his second family and experimentation with sex and pot. When he was fifteen, derisive of girls and struggling with drugs, he said point-blank, "Why didn't anyone pay attention?"

With twelve-year-old Lorena, who had always been "Miss Style," the subtle changes in her appearance should have tipped the adults off. It wasn't multiple piercings, or her Goth manner of dress, which made her look like she had stepped out of an episode of *Charmed*. Rather it was the fact that she seemed to be taking less time with her hair, which was her most striking feature. It was medium length, blond, thick and curly, and she'd sometimes come in wearing it up, sometimes in dread-locks, sometimes adorned with bright red streaks. Suddenly, that stopped. Her hair looked kind of messy, as if she was unwilling to spend time on it. Lorena also put up more of a fuss about going to family functions and to church, becoming slightly less available to her parents. Where she had been an A− student, her grades went to a B or B+, respectable, but not up to her usual standards. She turned in her as-signments and school projects, but spent less time on them. Again, look-ing back, these little changes were a prelude to her becoming sexually active and a heavy cigarette smoker.

In Frank's case, before he started smoking a lot of dope and got into the more serious trouble at school, cheating on tests and cutting classes, he gave up things he used to love. He didn't want to continue guitar lessons. He quit karate. He procrastinated more around schoolwork and chores at home. Mona, his mother, dismissed these things about her son—all adolescents slack off a bit, right? But Jack, his father, had a gnawing feeling that *something* was going on with Frank. Jack didn't trust him, but, knowing he was a worrier anyway, he was afraid to voice his concerns. He was also afraid of pushing Frank even further away, or making him feel overprotected, "like a sissy."

The truth is, had Jack relied on his instincts, communicated his con-cern to Mona, and the parents then laid down new expectations, it would at least have led to a discussion. Sure, Frank might have blown up at them. Regardless, the explosion would have provided them with an opportunity—a stop-action, so to speak—to talk about what was going on. And then their son might not have fallen into the deep hole that he later found so difficult to climb out of.

Remember that the goal always is to strengthen the empathic enve-lope by sustaining the connection with a child, which you can do only if you know him or her. Far too often, parents and other adults pay attention *after* so many potential links have been broken, and by that time, it's hard to reconnect. So, ignore the old guidelines that tell you that teenagers need "space." Be clear about what you expect, and take heed when those standards are not being met.

Sweat the Small Stuff

Sometimes it's a parent, sometimes a teacher, a coach, or a guidance counselor who first notices that a child is slipping. Here is a checklist of small expectations that all responsible adults should heed. Bear in mind a child's baseline. For example, if a child always handed in homework on time, even missing a few assignments indicates a small, but significant, change. However, with a child who rarely hands things in on time, it's important to assess whether she has gotten worse. If your child always ate voraciously, but now dines with slightly less enthusiasm, that's reason enough to pay attention. But if he was a picky eater to begin with, use that as a baseline to gauge whether he's more so now.

Small dips in school performance—grades go down a half to a full grade; doesn't put as many fine touches on homework; no interest in doing extra-curricular projects; increased procrastination.

The room—neat kids become sloppy; disorganized kids become even more so.

Personal habits—doesn't bathe as often; less care in daily grooming; goes to sleep later and/or has trouble getting up in the morning.

Appetite—subtle changes, as in, the child still eats but not with the same gusto, nibbling instead of wolfing it down; or binge-eats a particular food—now it's a pint of ice cream instead of the usual bowlful.

Friends—change in composition of core group of friends; starts hanging out with new kids who aren't producing as much in school, whose grades are a little lower, although not necessarily bad or marginal kids.

Activities—second-family involvement with TV, video games, and on-line activities captures more of their attention; the usual two hours a day turns into three or four.

Rewards and Consequences—aka Bribery and Punishment

In most cases, clear expectations and accountability, even if tempered by greater empathy, aren't enough to keep a child safe within the boundaries of the empathic envelope. That's why bribery (and punishment) is usually necessary as well. It may be counterintuitive to think of this prescription as a way of teaching modern teenagers how to have better judgment. It may sound distasteful, even ethically wrong.

More than a moral issue, though, our aversion to bribery and punishment is rooted in the fact that many of us are afraid of our kids. We're afraid of actually taking anything away. We often try to make deals: "If you don't clean your room, you can't go to Johnny's house." But then we fail to follow through, because we fear that our children will hate us for denying them, or because we fear that we'll ruin the little time we spend with them, or both. A result of such misgivings is that kids tend to feel *entitled* to have all the fun and material possessions they want—again, without making the effort to earn them, or having the fear of losing them.

Incentives, in particular, serve a dual purpose in contemporary life: by rewarding teens with or depriving them of the things and privileges they want, we motivate them not only to learn, but to stay connected to us. In fact, a rule of the new adolescence is that *kids will stay connected to adults and interested in what they have to say, at least until they get what they want.* Then, by the way, something else they covet— a concert, a party, a sleepover—will immediately appear on the horizon. The constant hunger teens feel for the next event, fueled by the techno-driven hype of the second family, can be used as a way to strengthen the envelope, rather than just weaken it. Thus, whereas a sense of entitlement leads to kids' devaluing adults, incentives and consequences inspire them to keep adults on their screen. They *need* us to earn what they'd like. This connection is vital when so little holds teens in the first family.

I first rediscovered incentives and negative consequences in conversations with principals and high-level school administrators who had tried various "packages" to teach morality, judgment, emotional intelligence — many of which, if implemented without consequences, failed to be effective. As a number of high school principals said to me, "We go to conferences all over the country. Experts discuss the pros and cons of these programs, and we finally have to admit that the only way we can help teenagers learn how to make thoughtful decisions is to include clear expectations and offer them what a layperson would call bribes and punishments." In a different language these veteran principals were reaffirming the balance between empathy and expectations central to this book.

"Label it what you will," he added, reading my mind, "an incentive, a reward, a bonus — this is what gets kids to pay attention to us, rather than just the peer group or pop culture — and to think about what's right."

Clearly, the notion of using the next big event in an adolescent's life as a "carrot" is a tactic increasingly employed by millennium parents, teachers, group leaders, camp counselors. Being a modern psychologist, it's not easy to suggest this retro-sounding bromide. But dealing with teens it's impossible to ignore a chance to create more traction with adults. So, if Johnny wants to go to a wrestling match next month, he has to stop the back talk between now and then. If Jenny wants to host a pajama party, she needs to keep her room clean for two weeks. If Johnny and Jenny want to stay on the track team, they need to maintain at least a C+ average.

When I present this idea to a parent group or at an in-service workshop for teachers, I invariably face a sea of surprised faces. Some find the notion distasteful as I said, especially coming from an "enlightened" psychologist. Why would I suggest a correlation between a boy's insolence and giving him permission to go to a wrestling match? One has nothing to do with the other. Doesn't the punishment have to fit the crime? And shouldn't we expect certain behaviors from our kids *without* having to reward them for it?

Again, those are all old-think assumptions. Parents and educators have been bombarded by several decades of developmental theories. Many of them are out there searching for exactly the "right" punishment. Is it fair? Does it fit the crime? Is it age appropriate? Meanwhile, adults are frequently so busy pondering such questions, paralysis sets in — and nothing is done. Besides, we now know that the punishment must fit *the child and adult*. Consequences work only if you know a child (What does he or she really want?) and yourself (What can I really enforce?). *Consequences must touch a child and must be enforceable.* This creates connection — a pause in the action that brings adults into the foreground and diminishes the extraordinary gripping power of the second family.

Remember: Teenagers always have some next big thing that they want — permission to go somewhere, to buy something, even just to hang out. Threatening to take away a favorite TV weekly program or denying access to E-mail gets their attention a lot faster than yelling the same old invectives. What's more, bribery and/or enforceable punishments also create that pause — time to really talk — which, in turn, motivates teens to step back from the second family and take more seriously the first family at home.

Michael, master of excuses, was way behind in his work by the end of his sophomore year. He ended the second term with two incompletes. For the first half of that summer, there were endless groundings and lectures and ineffective threats from his parents. The papers still weren't getting done.

In June, his mother, Amy, changed the dance. "I knew he wanted to have a big beginning-of-the-summer bash at the house. It was a given, something we'd let him do in the past. He and his friends always looked forward to it. I told Michael that the only way I'd let him have the Fourth of July party was if he finished the two outstanding term papers *first*."

"Hey, I *always* have that party. Are you *bribing* me?" a genuinely shocked Michael said (apparently having read a few parenting articles himself). "But . . . you know that it wasn't my fault that those papers didn't get done. I had computer problems."

For a moment, that gave Amy pause. Maybe she wasn't being fair. How was the party connected to school performance? What would bribery teach? Wasn't Michael entitled to some fun? In the end, though, she stuck to her guns. "I knew he wouldn't want to let his friends down, and I had tried just about everything at that point."

Needless to say, Michael finished his term papers. Not so incidentally, and this is key, that summer was one of the most harmonious the family could remember. For the first time in several years, Michael and his mother *talked*. They discussed his experimentation with drugs and talked about his new girlfriend, whom he was having some difficulty understanding. Michael discovered his Mom wasn't such a bad listener. Amy saw the other side of her son's face and realized he wasn't just a lazy goof-off. The balance between empathy and expectation had improved—and so had Michael's connections at home.

Cheryl's mother, Harriet, accidentally stumbled on a serious second-family problem when she implemented enforceable consequences for an everyday issue. She had literally tried everything in the books to put a stop to her daughter's unremitting hostility toward her younger sister—not getting involved, letting them work it out themselves, spending extra one-on-one time with Cheryl, and many other techniques she'd read in parenting how-tos about sibling rivalry. Finally, in a moment of frustration, Harriet blurted out, "The only way you can go to the 'N Sync concert with your friends is to not rag on your sister for the next week." Because Cheryl lived for concerts—and this, in particular, was one she was *dying* to attend—Mom definitely got her attention. Bribery or not, Mom's use of second-family lure stopped the action. Now Cheryl had a reason to be nicer to her little sister. Miraculously, peace reigned in the house for that week and several more.

More miraculously, Cheryl (in an effort to first talk Harriet out of punishing her) started to reveal how unloved she felt in comparison to little Tess who was, in truth, undeniably adorable and engaging. These discussions soon moved to Cheryl's everyday relationship problems with peers, an area from which she had pointedly excluded her mother . . . until now. Disturbing issues were raised—how the boys constantly ragged on Cheryl about her "big" breasts; her inability to tell whether they were looking at her or her body; and, finally, how she'd been groped and flashed by some strangers on the bus. Cheryl also hinted that she'd been smoking marijuana, but refused to fully admit it.

After a few weeks of asking, Mom faced her daughter's continued stonewalling with a simple choice: "Go to the doctor and be tested — for everything — or you won't go to *any* concerts the rest of this school term." Cheryl, sensing her mother's determination, wanted to be at these events more than anything. She furiously agreed. Her subsequent open discussions with their supportive physician, along with blood work and exams, lifted the curtain on Cheryl's true activities: she'd been smoking enough pot to make a drug counselor was necessary. All this began with a simple act, laying out incentives and consequences that created traction between this increasingly distant mother and daughter.

Call them what you will, but incentives and consequences are necessary in the classroom, too, as Mrs. Arnold, a seasoned sixth-grade teacher, demonstrated. Over her thirty-year career, she had witnessed children becoming progressively nastier to one another. Their language and cruelty appalled her and, finally, she decided to entirely abandon the usual academic curriculum. For one week Mrs. Arnold concentrated only on getting her students to stop calling out, interrupting, and insulting one another. Their incentive? If they didn't demonstrate that they could treat each other with greater respect — stop the name-calling, the teasing about looks, the cursing — there would be no sixth-grade play at graduation, a long-held and much-loved tradition. Believing Mrs. Arnold meant it, the kids tried harder. And, the more they practiced being civil, they not only succeeded at being nicer to one another, they also began to open up to her. Some kids talked about why they teased; others confided in her about feeling ostracized and bullied. In the end, this wise teacher had created incentives to behave better *and*, at the same time, motivated her children to open up, thereby strengthening her connection to them.

In another school, bullying had reached epidemic proportions. In fact, one child actually left the school because of relentless scapegoating. The administrator had tried several new empathy-building programs. Excellent though these were, the merciless taunting did not significantly decrease. Why? It was not a *balanced* approach — the expectation side was too weak. Finally, the school revised its strategy. They continued teaching empathy, but also adopted a tough new "zero tolerance" for aggression. Suspensions and withdrawal of privileges would now be added. This balance between incentives and consequences worked. The kids finally saw the adults were serious. They felt both respected by the grownups and respectful toward them. In other words, greater connection between the generations was created.

Do bribery and punishments lead to miraculous conversions? Absolutely not, but they usually lead to change. For instance, did Cheryl become a perfect daughter? Not necessarily, but at least she was learning how to practice more restraint, at home and in the second family of peers. Did Michael become an eager student? No, but he saw that when he had a goal, he could work for it. Did the kids in Mrs. Arnold's class become little angels? No, but the incentive program proved to be the turning point that year. The cursing and back talk diminished and some parents even reported seeing a change in their kids at home. Subtle as they were, in each of these instances, lessons *were* taught. The adults' actions had an impact.

Traction between adults and kids was created.

Incentives are necessary in a world built on instant gratification and a sense of entitlement—values reinforced by the second family, which create a slippery distance between grownups and kids. Adults need to keep in mind that kids don't even see us and certainly don't "get it" when we simply try to teach. Our messages are lost in the distractions of the second family. The idea of earning or losing freedom just about always creates more connection and respect in the empathic envelope. After all, every teen has in the wings another critical event that *must* happen. This is both the angst and the thrill of adolescence—it is forever alive with anticipation.

Applying the Same Expectations to "Fun"

When we think of expectations for kids, typically our minds drift to limits and standards of behavior. Kids should do well in school. They ought to be respectful to adults. They must be honest. They must extend themselves to others. We rarely extend our expectations to kids' amusements and to what they do in their free time. Unless it's something outright dangerous or objectionable, we almost never think in terms of monitoring kids' "fun."

We ought to.

One of the most unfortunate aspects of the second family is that pop-culture fare crowds out so-called old-fashioned interests, like hobbies and crafts, music lessons, and other pursuits that require patience and hard work. Given the plethora of frustration-free activities available to teens, who wants to practice boring scales or even show up at an appointed time for karate instruction? Many second-family devotees have trouble mustering the internal fortitude to sustain focus on anything that puts them in beginner's territory—repetition, mistakes, disappointment, and only gradual progress.

Kids even know this about themselves. A thirteen-year-old boy talking about his friends told me, "You know, I talk to my friends, and they'll listen for a second, but if something else catches their attention, they're gone." An articulate fifteen-year-old said to me in all seriousness, "I don't know what's happening to my generation. We're great, but we can't seem to focus on one thing."

The rise of the second family has precipitated a decline in childhood passion—by which I mean any kind of sustained, abiding interest that comes from within, not from the pop culture. I see this sad fact in one youngster after another: kids hit adolescence, and they lose interest in extracurricular activities that once had meaning and in which they were gaining mastery, like a sport or music lessons. Darya, twelve, a budding gymnast since age eight, informs her mother that she "has no time" for classes now. She prefers to watch her favorite TV shows and hang out on-line. Thirteen-year-old Derek, who was well on his way to a brown belt in karate, has become so involved with his peer group and their Friday-night gatherings, he is no longer willing to get up early for Saturday morning synagogue services. Rebecca, a straight-A student, always loved school and took piano lessons, until she hit thirteen and became a pop-culture freak. Now she drags her mother to TV shows and rock concerts and waits at the backstage door for the autographs she collects in an album. This is her new passion.

When I suggest to parents that they must broaden their standards beyond everyday matters of discipline to include what their children are doing for fun, they look puzzled. And when I say they must literally *demand initiative* — insist on kids developing at least one interest outside the second family — they are shocked. The idea of "forcing" a child to develop an interest is anathema to most modern adults — and, at first blush, it also seems impossible. Mothers and fathers (ironically, sometimes the same ones who tend to overschedule their children) are apprehensive about seeming too authoritarian. They're afraid that their children will react negatively to the idea: "But this is what kids are like in adolescence," one mother insisted. "My daughter already resents demands — my insistence will only make things worse," speculated another.

Of course, there's some truth in parents' concerns. Kids *do* initially balk. "I have no time," "This is unfair," and "I'm too old to be told what to do" are typical responses. Yet with just about every family I've worked with, when parents began to insist that their child chose *one* extracurricular activity that requires a bit of effort, the effects are far-reaching.

The Ripple Effect of Passion

More than a matter of a child becoming involved in something other than the second family, having a passion has a range of side effects. Besides removing the child from the bosom of the second family, even if it's just for a few hours a week, passion builds self-esteem and character, fosters heretofore missing relationships with other adults — coaches, teachers, mentors.

When a child develops sustained and rich interests, it strengthens first-family relationships and naturally creates better balance. Parents become more than chauffeurs and loan officers. They get to know the other grownups who help their children, as well as teammates and fellow enthusiasts. Parents themselves often develop a genuine interest in the sport or activity. You need only watch some soccer moms or parents at a recital to see the look of satisfaction. It's not just that they're proud of their kids, they respect them. They see how the hard work pays off. In turn, their children recognize the support.

The Dos and Don'ts
of Adult Involvement

I've learned from the kids themselves what they'd like their parents, teachers, coaches, and counselors to know:

Do learn about, get involved, and become part of the routine.

Do ask sophisticated questions that show your interest and knowledge.

Don't push too hard or applaud too eagerly. (As one kid told me, "I tell my mother to cheer inside — don't yell and don't stand out.")

Don't overschedule.

Don't insist on a class too advanced for your child.

Don't buy sophisticated equipment until your child is ready for it.

Insisting on a passion unrelated to the second family keeps some kids out of therapy and sometimes even saves lives. Jesse, for example, evidenced a list of subtle signals of trouble at age twelve. He was having problems at school and was becoming a Jerry/Ricki/Maury talk-show addict — so preoccupied with his looks and reputation that he was starting to push himself on girls sexually. At thirteen he was caught in the act on a school camping trip — convincing a semi-willing girl to, as *this thirteen-year-old* casually put it, "go down on him" right next to one of the tents. Thankfully, the school did not treat this event casually. Jesse was suspended. Now in family counseling his mom and dad made this ultimatum—pick one non-pop-culture area of interest and stick with it. After he unsuccessfully bargained to be manager of the girl's volleyball team (a favorite of many marginal second-family boys), Jesse reluctantly chose the soccer club. Being part of the club encouraged him to focus less on his sexual reputation and more on his natural athletic ability. Soccer also helped Jesse make friends who were similarly committed. He still swaggered and boasted, but began applying his bravado more toward soccer and less in the sexual arena. Soccer practice also broke his talk-show habit and kept his parents front and center—demanding their involvement in games, parties, traveling arrangements. This is a boy who definitely would have drifted way out into the second family, and gotten more deeply involved with casual sex to stave off feelings of insignificance. Instead, Jesse just missed potential danger; in the process, he stayed infinitely more connected to his parents and constructive passion.

With Rhea, who was shaken by the tragedy of her brother's death (page 138), I explained to her mother, Tina, that in order to reel her daughter in, she had to insist on Rhea demonstrating initiative. Despite her own skepticism, Tina subsequently told Rhea, "You *have* to pick one thing to be involved in."

Rhea looked at her mother as if Tina had spoken to her in a foreign language. She sputtered and complained, but when she saw Tina wasn't backing down, Rhea realized she had no choice.

Ultimately, Rhea picked photography because she liked to observe people, and she enjoyed the solitary work in the darkroom. It was also something she had once shared with her favorite uncle, and she ended up spending more time with him—deepening a relationship with this older man, which was particularly important with no father in the home. By sticking with her new hobby, Rhea realized she had a good eye, and she became increasingly proficient. That summer, unprompted, she signed up for a painting course, too. Those periods of separation from the second family enabled her artistic talent to flourish. She had finally tapped into an interest that came from a deep place within her, rather than from the pop culture. Not coincidentally, her mood began to lighten up in the bargain.

■

In the final analysis, strengthening the empathic envelope in these ways won't keep the second family out—that's not the goal anyway. But they will help keep children's involvement with the pop culture and peer network under control. Adolescents will still lie to their elders, exasperate them, and do what they can to avoid adult interference. But there's a good chance that the strategies I offer in this chapter will cut down on the nonproductive adult/child dances that create a destructive distance between you and your teen. Chronic distance has the power to turn experimentation into addiction, flirtation into promiscuity, self-consciousness over appearance into eating disorders or self-mutilation.

Not bridging the distance between the adult world and the second family is indeed serious business—such high psychological stakes, in fact, that it's also important to remember that isolated adults can't do this on their own. Whether we're talking about parents at home, teachers, coaches, and guidance counselors in schools, camp counselors, or clergy in houses of worship, to ensure that kids are protected from the innumerable dangers inherent in today's world, it's vital for grownups to create partnerships with one another. Responsible adults must devise ways to share information and to cultivate a network that accomplishes what none of them can do on their own: keep a watchful *collective* eye on kids, and, in doing so, expand the empathic envelope. In some cases, such partnerships can truly prevent tragedies from happening.

To be sure, the need for adults to come together for the sake of protecting children is the most critical issue facing twenty-first-century parents and all adults who deal with youngsters. It is also one of the most difficult. Questions of confidentiality, legality, and responsibility stump parents and educators alike. Many adults recognize that they're unaware of what's really going on in their kids' lives, they'd like help, but they don't know where to turn. There are absolutely no guidelines. We need to change the paradigm, to build bridges that enable all adults who deal with children to support and inform one another. In other words, *to create a force at least as powerful as the second family*. Hence, in the final chapter of this book, I will explain how to build such bridges, coordinate our efforts, and develop guidelines around difficult issues that all adults must address.

· 8 ·

"Don't You Grownups Ever Talk to Each Other?"

Creating Adult Partnerships to Protect Kids

In many communities, the second family has become stronger than the adult network. Parents and teachers work diligently at becoming more effective with children, but they do so in their respective spheres—disconnected, disgruntled, and, often, distrusting of one another. A new paradigm is called for in which adults widen the empathic envelope by creating partnerships that reach across this great divide, heal the schism, increase communication. In this way, they will be able to develop programs that truly reflect the needs of today's youth.

Dear Dr. Taffel

If I had a "Dear Dr. Taffel" column for parents, administrators, and teachers, some of the letters I'd receive would be:

Dear Dr. Taffel,

A boy in my class, who was once a fairly good student, has been handing homework in late. Normally mild mannered, he frequently gets into arguments with other kids. It's two months until Open School Night. I don't want to *alarm* the parents or make them feel as if I'm *intruding*. Should I call them at home?

Perplexed Teacher

Dear Dr. Taffel,

A friend of my daughter's has lost weight and seems very depressed. She's a dear girl, and I'm worried about her, but I don't want her parents to think *I'm meddling*. How can I deal with the situation?

Worried Parent

Dear Dr. Taffel,

I'm *caught between* the parents in my school who think we're not doing enough to uncover drug use at school and teachers who think this is parents' responsibility. Who's right?

Beleaguered Principal

Dear Dr. Taffel,

My son has been unmercifully teased and taunted in gym class because he's not a good athlete. The teacher tells him he has to toughen up. I'm afraid that if I go to the principal it will *make things worse* for my boy. So how can I help him?

Enraged Mother

Dear Dr. Taffel,

One of my seventh-grade advisees recently confided in me about an unchaperoned party the kids have planned over the Christmas holidays. We're not in school then, so I don't think it's my responsibility to let parents know. Besides, I'd hate to see this girl get into trouble *for being a rat*. What's the right thing to do?

Conflicted Teacher

Parents Versus Teachers

Parents, teachers, and school administrators face issues such as these on a daily basis, and although each comes from a different vantage point, they all have one thing in common: they have almost no idea of what to do. Beyond that common ground, however, the various adults who deal with children tend to face off in opposite corners. In one, you have parents, holding down the home front, struggling to contain and control their children, to keep them safe and to offer the guidance kids need to become caring and competent people. In the other corner are administrators, guidance counselors, and teachers of all sorts, managing school life, designing curricula, implementing programs and, in many cases, caring about the kids just as much as the parents do.

For their part, teachers blame parents for being lax at home and expecting the school to take up the slack. Educators feel like they have to clean up after too many parents—the same mothers and fathers who come to school and presume to tell them how to do their job. Teachers also feel that they're undervalued, unappreciated, *and* underpaid—yet parents always seem to ask them to take on more. Is it really part of a teacher's job to spot emotional problems or to deal with kids' special needs in the classroom? Besides, if an educator focuses on one child and misses problems in another, he or she may be open to a lawsuit.

Often (but not always), beneath these complaints is something few people acknowledge: a class conflict. Because teachers are so woefully underpaid, educators and parents may be at opposite ends of the economic spectrum. Particularly in urban and suburban schools with large numbers of middle-class and even well-to-do parents, teachers feel that mothers and fathers talk down to them, treat them like hired help, or baby-sitters. Interestingly, I've heard complaints about parents' disrespectful tones from teachers in less affluent schools as well. They feel that parents don't just discuss, they attack. And if educators do spot minor problems, parents get defensive.

Teachers frequently dread parent-conference days. They complain of parents muscling their way into the classroom, commenting on curricula, and denigrating the efforts of the school community. The way teachers see it, some parents are always on their backs, telling them what to do and yet few have constructive suggestions to give.

All this may be true, but there's a parent's side of the story, too. Even the most vociferous mothers and fathers report that they feel intimidated and shut out by many educators. From nursery through high school, parents tell me about their secret fear of teachers. The mere act of walking into a school often reminds them of their own powerless years as students. But it's also because teachers sometimes *do* circle their wagons and create an impenetrable boundary between home and school. Mothers and fathers resent that they can't discuss with teachers what they observe in their child at home. School consultant Michael Nerney offers this pungent observation: "Many schools seem to go out of their way to make parents feel unwanted—yet when something goes wrong, *then* they're invited in."

By the time children get to seventh grade, at which point classes are departmentalized, parents feel that twice-a-year conferences are a joke. Other than grades, which tell only a small part of the school story, they have no idea what their kids are doing for the bulk of the day. In the parents' view, Nerney is on target: teachers get in touch only when something serious or dramatic happens—cheating, blatant and repetitive truancy, not handing in half a year's worth of assignments, or being caught selling drugs.

Sadly, both sides are correct. Meanwhile, kids may go unattended because of this home/school schism. Instead of the adults communicating to ward off potential problems, the process is backward. No one talks until disaster strikes; then and only then do the two sides communicate in earnest.

Tom, an eighth-grader in Connecticut, was drinking every weekend with his buddies, but neither his parents nor any of his friends' parents knew about it. The whole gang was coming into school looking haggard, falling asleep in class, but the teachers either didn't notice or chose not to, and neither did the parents. It was business as usual, until Cairn, Tom's mother, became aware of changes in her son. She took it upon herself to notify several other parents. At this point, her son's friends turned on him, Tom explained, "because my mother got them busted."

In the end, Cairn emerged as the villain—and for the next several months her son continued to be ostracized. The school did nothing about this. Were it not for the fact that, with my encouragement, Cairn kept complaining to teachers, the guidance counselor, and the principal about her son being scorned by the other boys, the abuse heaped on Tom might have gone unnoticed. Finally, after six months of torment, the school suspended one of the main agitators, and the torture stopped.

"It was an unforgettable lesson to me," Cairn lamented. "If I ever see anything like that happening again, I'll keep my son out of it, and I'm not saying anything to anyone else. It nearly destroyed Tom—he felt so isolated, he almost had to leave school."

Confidentiality: A Cultural Quandary

Cairn learned a lesson she'll never get over. Part of the problem is that our dominant cultural ethos is: *Mind your own business.* Families are mostly isolated from one another. And what goes on within a given house is rarely witnessed or known outside those four walls.

It wasn't always like this. When I was a kid, parents and teachers had few doubts about "their business." If I back-talked the grocer, kissed a girl under a streetlight, or sneaked a cigarette, my parents heard about it from one of the neighbors by the time I got home. Few adults thought twice about reporting childhood misdeeds to a parent. Nor did the kids think there was anything odd or wrong about the system. I knew Mrs. Heller would not hesitate to tell my mother if she saw me hanging out on the street corner with my buddies too close to dinnertime. I never thought that the reprimand I received was Mrs. Heller's fault. I was the dumb one for being seen.

Times have changed. The checkout girl at the local Kmart certainly won't report on another teen—she'd rather die than talk to adults about kids' business. Adults themselves aren't much better. In this litigious society, we are disinclined to stop, to get involved, to offer an opinion, for fear of saying or doing the wrong thing. Professionals, including teachers, guidance counselors, even pediatricians, are often reluctant to share their insights, lest their judgments later be used against them.

When you consider the dicey behavior of teens nowadays, adults' reluctance to divulge what they know is understandable. For example, at a recent workshop for professionals, the topics that came up included: teachers overhearing tales of "gang-bangs" (sex, consensual or not, with a number of partners at once); a guidance counselor describing group lesbian sex; another teacher hearing about junior and senior high school binge-drinking at a recent party (translation—girls and boys *each* downing up to a dozen hard-liquor drinks); administrators being "sure," but unable to find hard evidence of older students selling marijuana to young middle schoolers; a dean becoming aware that kids were hoarding and selling their medications.

The basic question was always, "What should we do when we think something is wrong?"

Parents face a similar dilemma. We absolutely don't know when or how to talk to other parents. If another parent's child lies, is that our business? These are the same questions teachers and guidance counselors ask. When we see potentially dangerous behavior, do we call other parents? Tell other responsible adults? What is our "place"? What should be kept confidential, and what should be shared? It's not simply that we don't know what do to, we're often *afraid* to take action. And suppose we're wrong? Modern parents are just as skittish as professionals, walking on eggshells for fear of being ostracized, criticized, or worse.

Why Now?

Why is there such a great urgency to confront this issue now? The main reason is that we're living at a time when adults can become frighteningly disconnected from kids. As Planet Youth has become bigger and stronger, adult systems have been overshadowed. Where once parents seemed to have eyes behind their heads, mothers and fathers today are blinded by their frenzied schedules. Typically more connected to co-workers than to people in their own neighborhoods, they barely make use of the eyes in front of their heads. As a result, the empathic envelope is threatened; there's too little holding kids, keeping them safe. Sometimes, there's absolutely no one watching over them.

In addition, the circumstances around confidentiality are even more dire in light of the second family's code of silence. As I've pointed out, kids reluctantly confide in adults, and then only when a friend is literally teetering on the brink of disaster. *If the adults at least talked to one another*, scenarios such as the following might not occur.

In a Northwest school, the captain of the fencing team, an A+ student and, in many ways, a model citizen, hanged herself. Looking back on the tragedy, the teachers admitted that they had observed a subtle change in the tenth-grader's mood but none had ever thought to call home, or they were afraid that their interference might make the situation worse. Other parents also had noticed that the girl seemed a little off, but they were afraid of sounding critical of another parent's child.

In each of these cases, the adults simply never got together, never compared observations or shared with one another. Would that have changed anything? No one can know for sure, but it certainly wouldn't have hurt.

Widening the Empathic Envelope

Tragedies such as these over the last several years underscore the need for a dramatic shift in the type and degree of interactions between adults who are responsible for children's welfare. I was first aware of this problem in the late '80s when I wrote *Parenting by Heart*. I then suggested the creation of "peer groups for parents" — mothers and fathers forming information-sharing support networks (similar to their kids' groups of friends) *before* something bad happens. This notion struck a chord among isolated parents, many of whom called when the book was published and asked me to help them set up their own peer groups.

Around ten years ago, I was aware of the importance of widening the empathic envelope to include the school, but perhaps because my own children were just five and one at that time, I focused mostly on parent coalitions. Today, I have no doubt that peer groups for parents are more important than ever, but they must be integrated into a larger *parent-school alliance*. Over the last decade the value of these alliances has been proven to me time and again: when children's troubles are detected and adults communicate or share common strategies, tragedy may be averted.

I've even experienced the problem firsthand, when a friends' daughter, Tiffany, was in seventh grade. In Tiffany's class, one of her friends, Adam, had been talking for several weeks to his closest friends about feeling down. Though all his friends were worried, true to the second-family code, none of them told their parents or teachers. Finally, suspecting he might be suicidal, twelve-year-old Tiffany confided in her parents, my old friends Rick and Delilah, that she was worried about Adam. In the absence of concrete guidelines for dealing with such problems, even Delilah, a social worker, and Rick, an attorney—both knowledgeable professionals—had misgivings and asked my advice. What would happen if they called the school? What about the boy's parents? Would Tiffany be ostracized?

To be honest, I didn't have any quick answers either. Instinctively, Rick and Delilah knew they needed to notify not only Adam's parents but at least one of the adults who came in contact with the boy— administrator, guidance counselor, teacher, or coach. Since there was no structure in place to allow that kind of concerted effort to happen, their intervention was slow, hesitant, and almost too late. Thankfully, however, enough was done by the adults that Adam received the help he needed before acting on his depressed feelings.

In this and countless other situations, it has been painfully obvious that a peer group solely for parents wasn't enough. Near-misses like this convinced me that the parent-school schism needed healing. Through a series of focus groups over the last several years, I have been striving to understand the disparate viewpoints of each group and to encourage the adults to discuss, rather than destructively stew in, their discontent. I put pointed questions on the table. Some involved the everyday chain of command—how and to whom can a parent or teacher report potential problems, without fearing censure? Others concerned the mutual distrust and hostility—why such a schism exists, why so little information goes back and forth. What happens in junior high that makes the adult system break down even further? How do bureaucratic and legal concerns impact on the situation? Clearly, common problems were voiced at all levels—no time, no money, no contact, fear of lawsuits. Moreover, everyone agreed that kids' behavior had become so extreme that nothing less than a radical shift in both thinking and policy was required. But was there a way to attack these issues *together*?

Using insights gleaned from the earliest of those discussions, I began to help a number of parent groups and schools create partnerships that would ultimately change not only the way the adults conducted themselves but the way they regarded one another. The plan was to address the closed world of the second family, to increase adults' knowledge and understanding, and to know what limits were needed. *Our primary goal was to achieve at the community level the same balance of empathy and expectations I have advocated within families.*

Thus, it is not merely a matter of everyone agreeing to make the rules at home and at school more stringent, the consequences greater — that's only the expectation side of the equation. An educational component is also necessary, a system that informs and involves parents, administrators, guidance counselors, and teachers that, ultimately, fosters empathy for the children. Just as it's important for parents as individuals to gain a more realistic and intimate understanding of what is actually going on in kids' lives, so must a group effort increase educators' awareness and appreciation of the kind of painful everyday dilemmas teens face.

Unfortunately, as I observed a decade ago, it's usually serious trouble that prompts parents to break out of their individual isolation and seek support for themselves. This is true for the larger community as well. It often takes a crisis to motivate parents and school personnel to work together. Hence, many of the home-school partnerships I've helped or learned about in the past few years have come out of shocking tragedies. Moments of truth occur after a perfect student commits suicide; the entire basketball team is involved in a series of drug busts; a high school prostitution ring is uncovered; or a drunken boy wraps his car around a tree, killing himself and several of his friends.

I have hope, though. Throughout the country, significant movement toward creating these bridge-building partnerships is under way. (In the Appendix, pages 189–201, I include concrete steps culled from different programs.) These early steps represent a real paradigm shift, the beginning of what I believe will be a change in consciousness and in the way adults come together to create a community-size empathic envelope.

Piedmont Stories: How One Partnership Was Established

Creating a parent-school partnership can't be done in half measures. I've seen schools purchase various packages from outside consultants — for example, to deal with conflict resolution, anger management, or ethics — but they may fall short. Sometimes, the kids laugh them off. As one girl described a program that dealt with anger management, "It feels like someone's weird idea about the way kids learn these things." Much of the content in these programs is excellent, but they are ultimately not as effective as they could be, because most don't take into account the power of the second family. Or, programs are too narrowly focused — involving, for example, only teachers. For any coalition to create a strong empathic envelope, it must embrace the entire community and deal with the real world that kids inhabit.

It's best if it is a *formal* partnership, which, like the formation of any business venture, requires initiative, a set protocol, and commitment on everyone's part. This takes time — typically, two to four years to effect real change. Unless all parties proceed with caution, giving and receiving feedback along the way, there will be resistance. If so, the entire system may break down.

Naturally, parents and school groups have to create partnerships that reflect the problems and needs of their particular community. Still, there are a series of steps that seem to translate across the board. To illustrate them, I will use the example of Piedmont High School, a fictitious name that represents a composite of several real suburban and urban schools, where administrators and parents invited me to consult. Luckily, in these cases at least, the parents and school sprang into action *before* a major crisis had occurred.

Create a steering committee. A true partnership requires more than putting forth some vague idea of parent involvement. It cannot be a program run by an administrator, a special PTA meeting, or an assembly in which the principal merely lays out the school's problems and entreats parents to become more active. Therefore when Piedmont's guidance counselor first called me, I stressed that he had to immediately involve one or two strong parent leaders. Along with the principal, several key teachers, and coaches, those parents would be part of a steering committee that represented the larger community. In every matter they deliberated on, there must be consensus, and every step they took had to represent a joint effort.

Write a statement of purpose. The first business of a steering committee is to come up with a statement of purpose in which problems are identified and goals laid out. The mere willingness of all the parties and the act of coming to the table together is an enormous first step. At Piedmont, as in other schools I've worked with, taking this step alone produces a change in attitude. The process of converging from opposite sides is similar to what happens when marital partners who have been battling for years both become willing to see a counselor together. Having them agree to sit in one room, talk, listen, and respect each other is half the battle.

Likewise, with parent-school partnerships, writing a statement of purpose sends a message: The parents don't have to feel isolated; the schools need not be so distant and authoritarian. The statement will be different at every school, reflecting the unique concerns and ethos of that particular population. For instance, urban schools have different concerns from suburban or rural institutions. Cultural and ethnic makeup may give rise to particular issues, such as the need to address diversity. One school might be concerned about kids' drinking while another might choose to focus on teen aggression. Also, whereas one community might need to respect the liberal thinking of its constituents and take care not to impose policy too forcefully, another, conservative district might need to create a more hard-line statement that takes a very tough stance.

Spread the word, get feedback, and create an event. At these initial meetings, parents often voice universal concerns: they don't know their kids' friends and know less about how to deal with issues of confidentiality. Hence, one of the first orders of business is to raise other parents' consciousness and to get them talking. At Piedmont, the steering committee communicated with the larger parent body by mail and by making phone calls to interested parents, explaining the goals of the partnership. They also sent out questionnaires to gauge parents' attitudes and to assess, at least initially, their degree of willingness to participate.

Typically, six to eight weeks after this initial legwork is done, the steering committee conceives an event that involves the rest of the school. Their choice depends on what issues are pressing and what type of occasion will motivate parents to attend. The content of the evening might be teasing, drugs, sex, the difficulties of making the transition into high school, or whatever else emanated from the initial feedback. If the parent body is somewhat apathetic, the steering committee may invite a well-known expert as an enticement. If the school has fairly savvy, articulate students, the kids' input might become the focus of the first parent evening, as was the case at Piedmont High.

At Piedmont, the civics teacher, who sat on the alliance's steering committee, observed that all the issues they had identified boiled down to helping children make better choices, so he suggested asking *the kids* which decisions were toughest for them to deal with. Students in grades seven through twelve were assigned the job of writing short anonymous pieces about areas in which they clashed with their parents or situations they believed were important for parents to know how to handle. Not surprisingly, the kids' essays read like the "Dear Dr. Taffel" letters at the beginning of this chapter:

> A boy is being bullied by the other kids. You feel bad. You want to talk to your parents about it, but you don't want to get anyone in trouble. When you finally go to your parents for advice, what should they tell you?

> A girl has been keeping her eating disorder a secret. She has been binging at home, and she knows her parents hear her throwing up. She's getting worried. How should she handle it?

> I want to stay out later, because all my friends are. I told my mom, "I don't want to come home earlier than the other kids," and she

gave me a later curfew. But now my mother wants me to call her all the time, which is even more embarrassing than leaving early. How should my parents handle my wanting a later curfew when they don't feel comfortable about giving me one?

I have a boyfriend. We want to stay together overnight in my room but my parents won't let us. We're going to do whatever we want anyway. Why do they want us to do it in a place that could be dangerous, instead of my own house?

Working with each grade advisor, the teacher sifted through dozens of stories like these. The kids had posed insightful, albeit difficult questions. No adult could have isolated the problems any more articulately. This was a rare glimpse into their kids' world. Multiple copies of these "Piedmont Stories," as the essays came to be known, were printed and handed out at the upcoming evening event. This was the first time parents' involvement was welcomed at Piedmont. The mere act of cooperating on this project boded well for the partnership.

When you host the event, also educate about the alliance. At any function involving the school and parents, it's important for everyone to understand *why* building bridges is necessary. From my experience, parents and even teachers are abysmally uninformed about the second family and how organized it is. They need to realize that a similar kind of system has to be in place for the adults. All grownups, and ultimately students as well, must see this as a community-building effort. At the Piedmont event, before handing out the stories, members of the steering committee addressed the audience, explaining that this was not merely another assembly program but rather a joint effort through which all involved could help teenagers make better choices. By way of introduction, the principal and guidance counselor also talked a little about what the parents could expect from their kids in the year ahead: pushing for later curfews, getting together after school, sometimes in empty houses, and, in general, an increase in risk-taking behavior.

Break into small groups. After the new parents were welcomed, and the partnership introduced, the larger assembly broke up into small groups. Each was given several Piedmont stories and asked to discuss them. At the end, a group leader would report what had been said. With any large presentation, a more intimate forum is usually a good idea. When forming a parent-school alliance, this is especially important because parents and teachers have little history talking together and need the experience. Even parents with children in the same grade may not know each other. The idea is to get everyone to talk, grappling with the difficult situations and listening to one another's suggestions. This increases people's basic knowledge and, in turn, fosters empathy.

Assess the next steps. Generally, out of the first big meeting, the needs of all parties are crystallized. At most schools, it also becomes clear that participation must expand beyond parents on the steering committee. But the larger event is a good start—it brings out other mothers and fathers who might be willing to get involved. It also shows where the resistance lies. At one school, for example, few African-American parents attended, so the committee decided to hire a diversity expert to guide them through some difficult soul-searching and help them come up with concrete strategies that would get *all* parents involved. In another school, where kids commuted from long distances, some parents didn't show up because the school was too far away. It was then decided that subsequent evenings would be held at a more conveniently located church. Most important, this first big event proves to everyone that dialogue has to continue over the coming months. Piedmont's steering committee decided to have two additional large meetings over the school year. They started with parent-only gatherings and then moved toward assemblies with both generations in which they then broke down into parent-child discussion groups.

Involve kids later. Typically, when building bridges, students are at first peripheral. Involving kids before the adults have firmed up their relationships can be disruptive and divisive. You could invite teens and parents to an assembly on drugs or sex, but if the timing isn't right, they'll all be too uncomfortable—and no one will benefit. Remember that it takes time to make changes in a system. You don't want to incite a counterreaction in kids, who might feel like parents and teachers are organizing against them and decide to "outsmart" the grownups. They can sabotage the adults' efforts, or up the ante, which is exactly what happened at one high school. With the junior prom a few months away, the administration and parents made a joint decision to ban liquor. Unbeknownst to their elders, the kids scouted out a place to have a second after-hours prom, where beer flowed freely. The adults, of course, only found out after the fact.

Train parent facilitators and continue to have small group meetings. Once the ball is rolling, I advise parents and teachers of same-grade children to meet regularly in small groups—say, once every two months—among other reasons, to identify the ethos of their child's class. In any given school, every grade has a character all its own. For instance, at one school I visited, the seventh grade consisted of a group of really cooperative, academic-minded kids, but the sixth grade was riddled with problems. The girls were coming to school in seductive outfits; the boys were making life miserable for the "less-cool" guys. By increasing their connections with one another through ongoing meetings, the adults were able to identify issues and tailor their actions accordingly.

For small parent groups to be effective, however, parents (and teachers, if they volunteer for the job) need further guidance. After all, kids have plenty of experience talking in small groups, but adults don't. Parents sometimes don't feel safe with one another. A critical or self-righteous mother might say, "I don't understand why you have this problem. My kid tells me everything." Whether or not that's true is beside the point. Such a comment will definitely inhibit other parents from speaking out. When I worked with Piedmont, I explained that a parent facilitator has to understand the fundamentals of handling disruptive or monopolizing group members. They need to have guidelines about confidentiality, talking to one another respectfully and sharing information without humiliating one's own or another person's child.

One final bit of advice: Do not rush the process. Slow down and make sure that small-group discussions don't turn into gripe sessions about teachers and the school. These actually increase negativity and make it difficult for a partnership to gel. This happened in a town where peer groups for parents had been successfully instituted in a number of "sister" schools. In one school, though, the principal resisted the idea. She was concerned that her specific population of parents would use the groups to complain about difficult community issues as well as the school's problems. The organizers initially refused to heed the principal's warnings. But they soon discovered that she was right—several very aggressive and powerful parents had indeed helped turn the parent meetings into intense bitching sessions. Some of the parents even went home to their children to accuse them of things they'd heard at the meeting.

This is a lesson that should not be ignored by anyone involved in creating bridges between school and home. It is a clear-cut example of how an ethos of negativity combined with parents' unwillingness to respect rules of confidentiality—an important ground rule—can short-circuit the process. For parent groups to be effective, one must create connections between school and home that constructively fulfill the needs *of that particular group*. In this case, everyone would have been better served had they listened to the principal's wise assessment of the community.

Changing Policy

The most important and lasting effect of both small meetings and school-wide events sponsored by a parent-school partnership is the development of policies that address whatever specific and ongoing needs are identified. At Piedmont, and at other schools that create parent-school partnerships, at least one, but ideally all, of the following components of reform are instituted:

- A *witness protection program* that enables parents, students, and school personnel to confidentially report potential problems.

- A modification of the *parent-teacher advisory system*, which encourages parent and teachers to talk more easily.
- *Coordinated curricula* for adults and kids that reflect the values of school *and* home.
- *Zero-tolerance for everyday violence*, including teasing, bullying, ostracizing, and other forms of children's aggression against other children.
- Programs to *involve adults and children in good deeds*.

True and lasting transformation has a greater chance when parent-school partnerships incorporate these components. Below, I discuss them in greater detail.

Witness Protection: Hot Lines and Phone Trees

Of all the components of a solid and successful partnership, witness protection — a system that enables students, parents, and school personnel to report potentially dangerous situations — is among the most needed. As I've noted above, both parents and teacher, students and administrators, fear the wrath of the second family — ostracism and retaliation. People are not saints or martyrs; they need *help* in order to muster the courage to step forward. The biggest fear is, of course, the safety of one's child, but witness protection also allays adults' concerns about recrimination.

There's a long-term goal here as well: to change everyone's mindset — kids *and* adults. Kids don't want to go outside the second family. However, if their identity will remain hidden — *for real* — then teens who might otherwise be reluctant to betray their friends' privacy often come forth. And, when kids don't have to worry about the harrowing consequences of forthrightness, it helps them develop interpersonal ethics — a higher morality. They begin to recognize signals of distress in others, to feel some sense of responsibility, and to see that it's good to step outside yourself to help someone else.

In schools where students and teachers are offered witness protection,

I've seen serious dangers averted. For example, Mr. Smith, a dean of seventh-graders, began worrying as he watched Jill become thinner. Though the twelve-year-old was personable, friendly, and continued to get excellent grades, Mr. Smith noticed that Jill was missing a certain spark that had been evident since he knew her. Believing his intuition was on target, Mr. Smith turned to Jill's second family. In a careful way he mentioned his concerns to a group of Jill's closest friends, promising that confidentiality would be honored, but also stating very directly that if the girls knew that something was wrong, and if something happened, it would have been irresponsible on their parts *not* to help.

After agonizing for several days (but mentioning nothing to their parents), two of the girls came forward and told Mr. Smith that Jill was, in fact, becoming bulimic. She had been lying to all the adults in her life and to most kids, too. Only the closest members of her second family knew the truth. The girls admitted they had been afraid to step forward, because they were fearful that Jill's parents would be furious and make Jill's life even more miserable. Still protecting the girls' confidentiality, Mr. Smith consulted with the school psychologist and the two of them were able to enlist Jill's parents in a constructive intervention. Several weeks later, Jill and her parents were in family counseling. Her bouts of bulimia ceased and she seemed to be moving in a more positive direction.

In this and many other cases, a combination of empathy and expectation—as well as an ironclad assurance of confidentiality—opened the wall between adults and members of a child's second family. In Mr. Smith's school, "witness protection" was merely a guiding principle, a climate in which immunity was assured. However, it can also take a more concrete form—most often, an anonymous hot-line or phone tree. These are relatively easy measures to implement and they yield fairly quick results:

Hot lines. When a hot line is fully functional and effective, adults have to prepare themselves to hear information that will shock, even terrify. Like parents, who often wonder what they'll actually *do* when they find out what their kid are up to, some school principals and coun-selors admit they have mixed feelings about information that comes over transoms. "Do we *really* want to know?" they may ask.

If you're setting up an anonymous hot line, there are important con-siderations to bear in mind. Whether you utilize phone or E-mail, no system is foolproof or without its drawbacks. If a phone is used, where will it be? Who will have access? Will kids' voices be identifiable on an answering machine? If steps aren't taken to ensure that kids won't be singled out for making reports, the system will fail. *Of course, prank calls are inevitable.* And if E-mail is used, I've found that kids are even more likely to send phony messages and spread gossip about other kids. Still, once kids see a friend helped, the second-family mind-set begins chang-ing. Teens realize that talking to an adult *can* make a difference, and the pranks usually die down or stop altogether.

No doubt, though, hot lines can save lives. For example, one name-less teen called her school's hot line to report that a friend seemed depressed. Drinking more than a six-pack of beer, she had gotten wildly drunk, and began cutting herself. "I've seen this before. I know the signs," said the voice on the answering machine. Worried about her friend courting even worse danger than her already wild acting out, the slightly jaded teenage caller added, "I'm afraid *real* trouble is coming." The voice went on to say that she was afraid of what would happen if the girl's parents found out. "They're really crazy," she offered.

The teachers and the guidance counselor who heard the call paid attention. Even in this instance, the adults hesitated. They first discussed how they might deal with the matter of confidentiality, how to not make it worse for the child. They took into account the caller's fears that the girl would be punished instead of helped. By opening up the system in this way, they were armed with information and therefore able to take action. After brainstorming, they chose a dean who had a decent rela-tionship with the parents. He handled it very tactfully, taking into ac-count that the parents were considering divorce and were also financially strained. Their daughter, unbeknownst to them, was taking on their pressures.

For parents and teachers, a hot line can alleviate fears of trespassing onto each other's territory or that saying something about another child's dangerous behavior will negatively mark their own child. In one case, the mother of fourteen-year-old Sam had heard him talking to Neil, who had run away from home. Neil wasn't the victim of parental abuse; he merely wanted to be out from under their unusually strict rule (at least compared to many other parents in our culture). Now he was hiding from them, and none of the adults knew what was going on. Assuring Sam that he would not be implicated, Mom wrested information about the runaway's whereabouts. She called the school hot line, the principal called the parents, and, together, they figured out a compassionate way to get Neil to come home.

Phone trees. Another form of witness protection, particularly for adults, is a phone tree, a list of parents who all have one another's numbers, ideally at work, so kids are less likely to hear incriminating telephone conversations. In the best systems, teachers are also included. When these two groups communicate, kids can less easily play the adults off against each other, or finger any one adult as an informer. So, when the French teacher, Mr. Pardo, overheard the kids in his class talking about an unsupervised party in the planning stages, he immediately called one of the parents and activated the phone tree. Within a few hours, just about every parent in the grade knew the kids' plans and were able to discourage, if not forbid, their child from attending. In another school, a phone tree is used to alert other parents about which homes will be empty after school or on weekends. This doesn't stop kids from hanging out in unsupervised houses, but it *does* give adults more information to make informed decisions.

When teens first realize that their parents and their friends' parents are part of a phone tree, they are often suspicious and furious. "What right do parents have to find out what is going on in our lives?" demanded a group of kids in a Midwestern Quaker school. To which the parents, strengthened by their new connection, could say without anger or defiance, "It's our job to protect and take care of our children. We'll do whatever is necessary."

Getting Teachers and Parents to Talk

When teachers become comfortable alerting parents, and parents feel comfortable approaching teachers, it has a profound impact on how soon adults know that a kid is in trouble. However, the advisory system in most schools is often where distrust and discord between parent and teacher are most obvious. Ironically, both are tormented by the same doubts about breaking the code of silence.

In some schools, the homeroom teacher acts as an adviser or another teacher is assigned the role of handling general concerns and overseeing a child's progress. Either way, this person, who usually sees children fifteen minutes or a half hour after they leave home, has little or no communication with the parents. Even on Open School Night, moms and dads are more likely to hear reports from a student's classroom teachers about scholastic progress, but not from the one person who supposedly has the more holistic view of the child.

Making this situation worse, classroom teachers generally adopt a *don't ask/don't tell* policy about matters unrelated to academics. They believe their job is to teach, not to explore a child's emotional life. Besides, kids are resistant—who has the time to prod them into disclosure? Teachers are often even reluctant to call the guidance counselors—again, because of the extra time and the implications of getting involved.

Richie, fifteen, is in the midst of having fights with his first serious girlfriend. He's falling asleep at his desk, acts surly, and always has an excuse not to participate in gym, which he used to do with relish. Do any of the adults notice? If they do, they don't say anything. Weeks go by, and Richie's "bad mood" becomes unbearable. To distract himself, he ends up vandalizing and nearly burning down a house in a neighboring suburb.

Judy, who is ordinarily a good student, stops participating. Her grades have been slipping and she isn't as attentive in class. Teachers seem to notice but don't know what to do. Her friends are aware that she's partying more these days, but none of the adults are discussing the painfully obvious clues. Her acting out becomes so ordinary Judy marks her calendar a month in advance, to plan when her house will be empty so she can bring boys home.

Sometimes teachers don't get involved because they're afraid of making a situation worse. And, of course, that *can* happen. A teacher at a workshop told of calling a student's home because she was worried about the boy's depression, and during the phone conversation could hear mother and son screaming at each other. The boy did not show up at school for several days afterwards—plaguing the teacher about whether she had done the right thing. Obviously then, creating guidelines and support for teachers, is an essential task of school partnerships.

Breaking Down Teachers' Resistance

We need to notice small changes in kids' behavior, rather than wait until serious problems emerge (pages 144–148). This is true for teachers as well as parents. But along with a keener awareness, teachers need a set of protocols so that they know whom to talk to, who calls the parents, who follows up. Granted, there will be resistance: in many schools, teachers continue to insist that educating is about imparting a body of knowledge, not to operate *in loco parentis*. The antidote is to teach teachers: help them see that by spotting small problems before they become big ones, they will end up with more receptive students. When children are emotionally healthy, they're more available and infinitely more teachable.

Wise administrators, listening to the frustration of parents, sponsor mandatory in-service programs to raise teachers' awareness. Some proactive principals even arrange financial compensation for teacher participation. In one such high school program, the guidance counselor enumerated the early warning signals of emotional distress—and printed up materials about manners of dress, attentiveness in class, change in habits, and distancing from kids who were once friends. The counselor made it clear that she would welcome hearing from teachers; she set aside special hours and gave out an emergency number. Most important, the school administrators cut down on the paperwork needed if a teacher stepped forward. As the term progressed, the teachers naturally began to pick up on the signals *and* knew what to do. The invisible wall between classroom teachers and administrators started to disappear. This distance is, in many schools, one of the primary ways adults don't sufficiently communicate. Feeling the parents' and administration's gratitude, teachers became less reluctant to share information. In the end, everyone won.

School Lessons/Home Lessons

Too often, ideas promoted by teachers and counselors are lost as soon as a child gets home; likewise, parents' teachings are frequently not mirrored in the school environment. However, when the walls of distrust begin to come down, real progress can be made toward developing curricula that reflect values in both arenas — peer-group programs orchestrated at school *and* at home. Often, these efforts come out of one of those "big event" evenings organized for the whole school, which addresses specific issues, such as sex, drugs, or vandalism.

For instance, although parents are generally aware of the dangers of drug use, they need concrete information in order to understand and monitor kids' behavior. To that end, many school partnerships invite a substance-abuse expert to talk to the parents of eighth- through tenth-graders, a time when drug use is rampant. Most parents, who consider themselves quite knowledgeable, referencing their own recreational use in their teens, are shocked to learn of all the new designer drugs on the market. They are appalled to hear that a new method of distribution is not the stranger on some dark street corner, but, perhaps an older sibling. They learn that cigarette smoking, which many consider a fairly innocuous vice compared to other illicit temptations, is, in fact, a gateway drug.

More than just a matter of continuing education for parents, increased awareness helps spur new programs and change attitudes. Many realize that if you want to make an impact on drug use, it's not enough to just say it's wrong or even warn kids of the consequences. You must also educate and understand their plight. As a result of one such lecture, an English teacher assigned essays on cigarette smoking and, as part of the homework, directed kids to anonymously share these with their parents. This was her way of helping adults understand what it is like to be a kid in today's world, what teens are up against, what tempts or repels them. The administration, realizing that parents wanted them to get tougher, initiated suspensions and expulsions for using or, worse, selling drugs. The principal later admitted he'd never have had the courage to take such a strong stand on his own; he might have feared parental resentment. That evening ultimately led to a series of others on high-risk behaviors, but now parents, teachers, *and* kids were on-board.

When parents and teachers feel like they're in it together, they are better equipped to evaluate curriculum needs and, if they decide to bring in outside experts or purchase "teaching packages," they are more likely to choose wisely because they grasp the problems at a much deeper level. In the school I mentioned earlier, where the sixth-grade girls were dressing so provocatively, a series of small-group meetings determined that sexual harassment had become an issue. The girls were both suffering and being titillated by the boys' innuendoes. The taunting wounded some and made others feel left out. Had their been no parent-school partnership, perhaps this situation would have been left unattended, written off as something the kids had to go through—an ordinary part of growing up. Instead, parents and teachers began reading material on gender issues, discussing it, and seriously looking at what this kind of mistreatment meant to the girls *and* the boys. They realized that even though sexual harassment may be part of the culture, they didn't have to ignore it. Out of those small-group discussions, two programs were created: one that helped the parents see what their kids were up against and taught them how to talk to their kids about the problem, another for the kids to help them to understand the impact of such talk and also how to field harassing remarks.

At another school, when a tiny twelve-year-old girl drank so much alcohol at an unsupervised party she had to have her stomach pumped, the parents and administration suggested a "safe house" contract. In signing, the parents promised that an adult would always be present when adolescent friends got together at their homes, that no child would ever leave the premises at night alone, and that no alcohol would be served or tolerated.

Even though there wasn't across-the-board involvement, mothers and fathers felt bolstered by knowing who supported the idea, and by having more information on which to make decisions. And teachers who once complained about being baby-sitters could now identify which parents knew and supported a set of concrete guidelines for the kids' burgeoning social life. (See a sample safe-house pledge on page 193.)

Just Say "No" . . . to Everyday Violence

In the wake of incidents like Columbine and far-less-dramatic examples of school violence, perhaps one of the most important outgrowths of parent-school partnerships is the recognition that adults must not tolerate various forms of children's aggression toward one another. We can't expect everyone to like one another, but we can dictate new standards of social behavior, enforceable at home and in school. These are related to what I call "everyday violence"—the taunting and teasing we often take for granted. Fortunately, many schools have already begun to shift their perspective from viewing openly and consciously cruel behavior in school children as "normal" to seeing threats, ostracism, and bullying as so damaging they may require punishment. Typically, programs try to help children understand both what it's like to be the object of taunts and what it means to be and think like an aggressor.

Hot lines and telephone trees can help bring this behavior out into the open, but unless parents and administrators adopt a zero-tolerance policy and take a hard line when it is breached, the aggression will continue. Consider what happened with Terry, who had been receiving anonymous E-mail that literally threatened her life: "Come to school and you will be killed." A harmless prank? I don't think so. Terry was afraid to leave her house. Her parents, at first, feared contacting the school, because Terry might get into trouble. Terry and her friends suspected the culprit, but everyone was afraid to name names.

Luckily, this was a school that had begun to address everyday violence, and a movement was already under way to institute a hot line. One of the first calls identified the kid who had been sending Terry the threatening letters. The school called Terry's parents, who told the principal to take whatever action he deemed necessary. Emboldened by their support, the principal broke into the school's Internet system, traced the E-mails, and was able to prove that the boy who had been named on the hot line was, in fact, guilty. In addition to suspending him, the principal made him apologize to Terry and her parents for his behavior. It also became clear that not enough had been done to educate other students about this problem. By the following fall, the teachers were given a workshop on everyday violence and all students were required to participate in an antibullying program. The balance between empathy and expectations proved quite successful here, as in other schools.

Involving Adults and Children in Good Deeds

Too often, when we admonish our kids to "do good," we send them off on their own. They earn community service points at a holiday soup kitchen when they collect money for UNICEF, or help with a charity mailing. There's nothing wrong with expecting kids to give of themselves, but in this era of the second family, the gesture is more meaningful when teens join with adults and create intergenerational connections around good deeds. Sharing charitable endeavors provides a forum that enables parents and children to break through the boundaries usually separating their worlds. Connectedness comes out of collective caring.

It's best when charitable deeds are devised by parents, teachers, and students in each grade. This way, projects can be developed that are age appropriate. At Piedmont, for example, the sixth-grade kids and adults participated together in a Hunger Project. Through a tremendous amount of cross-generational planning, food was collected, prepared, and delivered to a neighborhood center. Everyone had fun doing it and, best of all, got to know each other in a less formal, less hierarchical setting. A few of the kids were actually better cooks than some of the adults, and it was great for them to reverse roles.

Debbie Spaide, founder of Kids Care Clubs, a nationwide organization with 450 chapters, describes school projects in which parents and kids reach out together to the elderly during the holidays, delivering Giggle Bags filled with items "to make someone smile." Other projects, Spaide suggests, that even middle school kids relate to are Pajama Days, when kids come to school in pajamas and donate their clothes to the poor, and Reading Robin Hood programs—when families gather childrens' books, donate, and read them to younger kids.

The possibilities are endless, but Debbie Spaide herself reports that getting adolescents and parents to work together is one of the biggest challenges of volunteerism. The two generations simply do not look to each other as potential partners, even for a good cause. To increase the possibility that such a high school program will work, remember these guidelines taken from many interviews:

1. Projects should be short—teens won't make long-term commitments.
2. Focus on an urgent need—teens need to feel needed.
3. Make the project hands-on—kids relate to concrete action and connections.

It is probably no accident that just about every partnership program begins with expectation, moves toward creating greater empathy, and ends up with good-deed-doing. The bottom line is that instead of giving lip service to the benefits of being charitable and sending kids "out there" to the community, adults need to join in. Actions are more important than words. Through these experiences, parents' and kids' attitudes toward each other change. Where once only the second family reigned, greater connection between adults and teens is created.

Will It Work?

Can I in some way statistically document that parent-school partnerships make a significant difference in our children's futures and in the way the various systems interact? Admittedly, it's too soon to tell. But based on increasing feedback I've received from both parents and school personnel, there is reason to be hopeful. The Appendix will offer concrete suggestions taken from a number of programs that have been running several years and have had truly positive responses. In general, parents feel empowered, teachers feel less defensive. Both sides are able to discuss thorny issues more openly and come up with solutions tailored to everyone's needs. And, slowly, some kids are joining with adults to tackle concerns that up to now had never been acknowledged.

In the final analysis, as we're beginning to see, it is life-saving to treat the school, the family, and the community as one large system and deal with the whole organism. In this way, everyone is on the same team; everyone acknowledges that he or she must be part of the solution. Indeed, it's no accident that I get one or two calls a day from people around the country who want to create these bridge-building partnerships.

This is an idea that comes full circle: an empathic envelope — balancing expectations and empathy — includes everyone in a child's life. When we seek this balance, we create a world that has some possibility of addressing the power of the second family. We create a "there" there, a place where we can pull teens back and make them feel compassionately held. As one grateful parent, who had finally found the right mix between expectation and empathy, said, "It's as if my child returned from a long, long journey to a very distant land."

We need to reckon with adolescent power; we need to deal with kids realistically to create greater connections and surer guidance. And, our efforts will only succeed if we offer a world balanced enough to welcome them back home.

Parent-School Partnership Initiatives
Specific Guidelines for Successful Programs

The Necessary Components of a
Parent-School Alliance

Experience in different communities suggests that parent-school alliances are "systems." It is therefore important to include the key aspects of the system. If one or two important components won't participate, the effort will likely fail. The key components are:

- Two or three highly proactive parent leaders.
- Representatives from administration — in particular, the principal and deans.
- Teacher representatives.
- Guidance counselors.
- Representatives from any health or wellness center connected to the school.
- Law-enforcement personnel involved with the school.

Tasks of the partnership:

- Conceptualize the needs of the community.
- Coordinate events.
- Get parents to participate.
- Evaluate the effectiveness of each event and the entire process as it unfolds.

Sample Mission Statement for
Parent-School Alliances

Every school-parent alliance needs to have a formal mission statement. Part of the goal is to increase the parents' and the schools' consciousness about where the process is heading. Although it may seem like a waste of energy, a mission statement that is acceptable to those involved articulates the reason for the partnership's existence. Each community needs to come up with its own, but here is a sample that can be used as a general guideline.

The alliance's goal is to protect our children and help them make smart choices about high-risk behaviors and other life decisions.

We will do so through a collaboration of the important adults in our childrens' lives — parents, teachers, school administration — establishing a process that will educate, increase mutual respect, and problem-solve.

We will strive to create the same atmosphere of honesty, empathy, and openness to diversity we wish for our children.

We recognize we are a part of a vital and interdependent community that is dedicated to self-examination and self-improvement, as well as the strengthening of a strong ethical code in adults and our children.

We understand that these are not simple goals, and commit ourselves to a process that will require patience, time, and the efforts of many.

For the sake of our kids and our community, you are welcome to participate in this alliance.

Getting the Money

The biggest problem facing parent-school alliances (besides time commitments), is raising sufficient funds. Each community deals with this issue in different ways, but it cuts to the core of whether there is true school and community support. Some of the more common methods to raise funds are the following:

- Write grants focused on prevention of high-risk behaviors. Many family foundations as well as not-for-profit organizations have become interested in preventing dangerous acting out by our youngsters. The money is there—if the programs you create are concrete and well thought out.
- Make connections to nearby universities. Research programs are interested in the "before" and "after" effects of these initiatives. This is particularly true for programs that center on high-risk behaviors such as alcohol, drug use, and preteen and early adolescent sexual behavior.
- Co-sponsor with health centers, hospitals, and churches in the community.
- Ask neighborhood businesses and national franchises to underwrite. Many corporations and local tradespeople are eager to contribute and to have their names associated with these kinds of projects.
- Sell books and other teaching materials of guest speakers who are experts in child-rearing and teen risk areas. This will offset the cost of the event.

Peer Groups for Parents: Guidelines for Effective Communication

These ground rules have been used by many parents groups and should be handed out at meetings, especially when a new group forms.

Don't:
- Interrupt each other when speaking.
- Criticize others for having a different point of view.

- Consider that your way must be the right (or wrong) way.
- Talk about someone else or a child who is not there.
- Return home to share, gossip, or accuse your child about information discussed in a group.
- Reveal anything potentially embarrassing to your child.

Do:
- Stay within the specified time limit when it is your turn to talk.
- Share information that increases other parents' knowledge of everyday life with kids.
- Reinforce each other's attempts to try new approaches.
- Respect differences of opinion, ethnicity, gender, and class.
- Choose readings or invite local experts to discuss child-rearing matters.

Considerations:
- The group must decide which discussions need to be kept just within the room. Most successful groups expect (promise to each other) confidentiality, at least regarding some sensitive topics.
- When kids first hear about peer groups for parents they often take an adversarial position, finding it offensive that parents, *not kids*, are networking. After a while, though, kids settle down and accept these groups as part of life.
- Many groups develop a core constituency. Often, the most troubled families are the ones who refuse to become involved. Efforts should be made to personally reach out to as many parents as possible. Reaching out slowly expands the group, in particular, when people start to hear good feedback about the meetings.

Guidelines for Facilitators of Peer Groups for Parents

Parents can be trained to run groups without the need for professionals at every meeting. This is cost-effective and empowers those involved. Brief training is always helpful—invite an expert in group process for a one-night workshop. He or she will strengthen the skills necessary to run a group. The most important are:

Always keep the goals of the group in mind:
- To increase empathy.
- To increase tolerance for differences.
- To increase active listening and the ability to communicate respectfully.

In order to reach these goals, facilitators should:
- Hand out the group guidelines before each meeting.
- Remind the group that the job of the facilitator is to keep the discussion moving and to create a sense of safety.
- When enforcing any do's and don'ts, the facilitator should refer to the guidelines, making his or her comments as impersonal as possible.
- When a participant is beginning to dominate and the meeting gets out of hand, intervene by taking turns; structure by going around the room so everyone is sure to get a chance to contribute; ask a quiet, nonparticipating member a direct question—if you think he or she can handle it.
- Tell an angry group member who won't stop talking that you will discuss the issue privately after the meeting.
- Do not criticize. Try instead to validate what each person says while leaving room for differences of opinion.

Sample Safe-House Pledge

Communities around the country are trying to adopt concrete standards for parents of teens. One of the most visible measures is a safe-house pledge. Most pledges, adopted as early as sixth grade, contain some or all of the following guidelines:

1. I will be responsible for the rules in my house, not my child.
2. I will not leave my home without adult supervision. If no adult

can be present during weekdays from 3 P.M.–6 P.M., I will ask neighbors to check in on my house.

3. An adult will always be present when a teen gathering or party is in progress.
4. I will allow no illegal substances, or accessible liquor, in my home.
5. I will not permit "crashers" (unknown kids) to attend parties held at my house.
6. If a child seems inebriated I will call his or her parent, or the parent of a friend.
7. If intoxicated, I will not allow a child to drive and I will call his parent(s).
8. I will call law-enforcement officers if a party begins to get out of hand.

Considerations:

- Some PTAs vote to adopt the pledge; other communities circulate the pledge and simply ask for signatures.
- What does one do about those who won't sign the pledge? Many communities feel that some compliance is better than none—and it is helpful to at least know which families are committed to the idea.
- Should the school administration make this an official policy or will it be initiated by parents? This depends on the level of cooperation established between school and home.
- If you are considering such a pledge, find out whether is it considered legally binding in your state. Specifically, does it make a parent more vulnerable and liable in case of problems?

School-Parent-Student Events

Knowing when to schedule a coordinated event that brings together the different generations is risky business. Why? The content of programs can be scary and embarrassing for kids and parents to discuss formally. Because of this, it's best to include kids *after* the parent-school alliance has gotten off the ground. Some of the most successful events that include both teens and adults are the following:

- *Health Day.* Different areas of health concerns are presented in many formats: booths, plays, discussion groups, videos. Parents and kids can choose which they want to visit.
- *Panel Discussions.* Volunteer kids can be part of a panel to "educate" parents about adolescent issues. Small discussion groups can then break off with parents sharing reactions to presentations.
- *Expert or Celebrity Assemblies.* Certain child-rearing experts and celebrities are able to bridge the gap between generations. They can discuss specific issues using their celebrity status in ways that encourage kids and parents to forget inhibitions with each other.
- *Specific Topic Days.* A couple of times a year the alliance can promote a morning devoted to a difficult topic. Sex, drugs, teasing, and so on can be approached by the different groups in school, who then educate and discuss with the others.
- *Intergenerational Fun Days.* Some of the most successful events are those built on having fun, such as concerts, picnics, and fairs. Literature and educational material is included as a backdrop. These events create goodwill and inform the community about the partnership's existence and goals.

Events Scheduling: A Monthly Guide

Attracting parents to building bridges events is often a matter of good timing. Issues are surprisingly seasonal. Here are some time-tested rules for attracting the parents of teens and preteens:

Early–mid-September. Don't bother scheduling an event, everyone is shell-shocked from the summer to school-year transition.

Late September–October. Teasing, ostracizing, and other social concerns are on parents' minds — the kids are beginning to form cliques.

Mid-November. School performance and discipline issues — report cards and school conferences have just brought problems to the forefront.

Early December. Stress — family life is beginning to fray as the holidays approach.

January–February. Drugs and alcohol — the holiday season has passed, and along with it, many kids have been exposed to a lot of alcohol consumption. They are also considering experimenting with drugs during the bleak, boring days of late winter.

March–April. Sex — spring brings with it the same old story, only wilder and younger. Between February and April, kids try "first-time" experiences at record levels.

First two weeks of May. Transitions — life is heating up with end-of-year deadlines, tests, and projects *and* the anticipation of summer vacation. Parents need help managing it all.

Ways to Encourage Parent Participation

The problem of getting tired parents to come out to events, on weekday nights or weekends, is a formidable one. Following are some typical and more creative ways partnership programs have increased attendance:

- Schedule events on a night parents need to be at school anyway, for example:

    School district election nights.
    PTA election nights.
    Special PTA meetings — e.g., PTA puts together slide or video highlights of school year, soccer-football seasons, proms, homecoming, etc., which showcase the kids. Parents love seeing pictures of their children — and will turn out.

- Coordinate the event way ahead of time to avoid conflicts, especially with sports scheduling.
- Do not rely on "backpack" flyers. Half won't get home. Instead, "multi-advertise":

    In-school newsletters.
    Flyers — mail flyers home.

Ask key parents to call others.

Create a phone tree *two weeks* before an event; this serves to remind busy parents.

- Provide child care—this increases the chance that more fathers, who would normally be at home with younger kids, will attend.

Student-Run Magazines

The information explosion has encouraged many students, who otherwise wouldn't have spoken out, to write their views in magazines or on Web sites. Recognizing this trend toward open dialogue, a number of schools have started high school news magazines that are minimally censored. Kids contribute articles, educating parents and other adults on a wide variety of subjects. Several high school magazines have run issues that include dozens of articles, some signed, some anonymous, written entirely by students. Among the topics are:

- Arguments for and against high school sex.
- Why kids smoke pot.
- The declining role of peer pressure.
- The distractions of sex versus schoolwork.
- The loss of childhood innocence.
- Sex for fun.
- Sex for love.
- When parents catch you in the act.
- Sluts and players.
- The allures and consequences of drinking.
- Drugs as a social crutch.

Besides the kids themselves, who are the most interested readers? Adults, of course. They see this as an unusual opportunity to learn kids' views on extremely sensitive issues, not easily discussed.

Parent-School Newsletters

The role of school newspapers has been changing. Because parents are so pressured and can't always make time to participate in ongoing groups, many schools have begun to use newsletters to share child-rearing information. Mothers and fathers know creative childrearing techniques that are often more effective than standard expert advice.

Consider adding a column (or several) in each issue of the school newsletter like these:

- 25 Ways to Build a Child's Self-Esteem
- How Different Parents Handle Curfew
- The Everyday Rituals We Still Do with Our Teens
- How We Handle Rudeness and Back Talk
- The Ways We Still Have Conversations with Our Teenagers

The possibilities are endless — but the goal is simple: parents from your community need to talk more with each other, especially to share ideas that work.

School-Run Parent "Support" Groups

Though I am not fond of labeling parent meetings as "support groups" (it sounds too illness and pathology based), I have found some proactive guidance counselors, social workers, or nurses to be gifted at getting parents together on a regular basis. Support groups may be a formal component of a partnership or offered independently by the school. Here are several guidelines that have proven successful:

- Groups are organized according to grade. Usually transitional years are the best place to start — sixth-, eighth-, and ninth-grade parents are particularly willing to meet with others.
- Once they coalesce, groups do not always admit new members. New members may be added when the next term of the school year begins.

- Groups meet as often as once per week, as little as once per month.
- Some schools divide groups, not according to grade, but "issues," such as post-divorce life, discipline problems, communicating with kids and so forth. These are usually short-term, theme-centered groups.
- Groups may continue for several years, parents moving up through the grades together. One group I know of met all through middle and high school, finally "graduating" when their kids did.

Creating Your Own "Peer Group for Parents"

Sometimes the school cannot (or won't) get involved with an alliance program. In this case you can begin a parents' peer group on your own. Use the experience of others who have been successful. Many write to me about the challenges of starting one and the unbelievable support they feel when it gets going.

- Start with people you know well. Try to choose parents from within your child's grade.
- Work from this core group and call as many parents as possible before the first meeting. Divide the task of calling.
- Always have light snacks, coffee and tea. Make the atmosphere as warm as possible.
- Use the guidelines for effective group communication following the "do's and don't's" on pages 191–192 of the Appendix.
- Limit the group to a size that is not too large and therefore inhibiting—usually eight to fifteen members.
- Occasionally invite local experts on specific topics to educate and give the group some authority.
- Choose books, videos, and other teaching devices to lend substance to group discussions.
- Follow meetings, especially at the beginning of the group's existence, with personal calls or cards thanking everyone for coming and acknowledging their input.
- Remind members of the next meeting. Ask them to RSVP if they

cannot make it. Establish a sense that the group must be treated respectfully.

- When a member goes through a difficult time, even if it's not directly related to a child-rearing concern, offer the group's support. This sharing and caring bonds group participants.
- At least once a year hold a "fun" event—barbecue, picnic, birthday, potluck dinner. The group is not just about difficulties, but about creating rituals and a sense of neighborhood.

If you cannot take this on independently, approach your house of worship or community center to establish peer groups for parents. Many already have them and many more are becoming open to the idea.

Problems Parent-School Alliances Encounter

The process is a difficult one, and vulnerable to setbacks. Fortunately they are fairly predictable:

- *Problem*: Alliance is dependent on one or two *charismatic* parent leaders.
- *What to do*: Begin searching for several replacements many months before their term expires.
- *Problem*: A tragic-event-precipitated partnership. Over time everyone forgets, or loses interest.
  What to do: Loss of interest needs to be offset by creating the *ritual* of several exciting events each year.
- *Problem*: The alliance and PTA may view each other as adversaries.
  What to do: This is common. The PTA, which traditionally serves as the infrastructure of school-home connections, must either promote the alliance itself or continue providing the glue for ongoing events. They cannot be snubbed or ignored because of this "new" idea—the parent body will fragment.
- *Problem*: A major school administrator, usually the principal, leaves his or her position.
  What to do: If a partnership program is established, it should have

some input into the process of finding a replacement. If this is not politically viable, the new administrator needs to slowly learn about the alliance, and over time, make it reflect his or her own particular vision. Parents must be open to new perspectives, since the partnership cannot survive without the principal's support.

- *Problem*: A major event unexpectedly draws few parents, and disappointment threatens the process.

What to do: This always can happen, and always has a good reason. Review the following to find out what could be done better next time:

> The event was held on a night that conflicted with too many other events.
>
> It was scheduled just before or after vacation time — parents way too stressed-out to participate.
>
> The topic was off-base — do some market research to get back on track.

- *Problem*: The alliance is causing resentment in school community.
- *What to do*: The organizers can sometimes become insulated from honest feedback, move too fast, or exude a sense of self-importance. Open the organizing group up to its more vociferous objectors, have less-ambitious goals, don't "get ahead" of important people in the community without their input — and most important, don't try to overshadow others who've worked hard for many years.
- *Problem*: Teachers are uninterested.
- *What to do*: This is primarily because of economics and job description. Teachers must slowly redefine their roles, and need incentives, sometimes financial, to participate. Teacher events should be scheduled just after the school day, so more will be around. Teachers must see immediate pragmatic benefits, for example, techniques to deal with problem children, ways to handle difficult parents, clear guidelines about whom to contact about dangerous teen behavior, and so forth.

Acknowledgments

My thanks to the kids, parents, and other child professionals who every day open themselves up and struggle along with me. You helped me learn what modern adolescence and pre-adolescence are about. As a parent myself, I deeply resonate with what other adults, responsible for teens' lives, go through. I am wiser (as well as much, much grayer) for it all.

My thanks to Lara Asher and Jennifer Weis. You had the courage not to back away from this difficult material. Your ability to "get" the raw, but balanced perspective of *The Second Family* is what made it possible. Lara, you in particular have been masterful at creating a collaborative, respectful relationship during the entire process. I thank you for being such a superb editor.

To my literary agent, Eileen Cope, of Lowenstein and Associates. You don't get excited by everything that crosses your desk. So when you reacted powerfully to *The Second Family* I knew we had hit the mark. I love having you on my side in this publishing process, one that often has less to do with writing than raw intelligence, judgement, and grit — you've got them all.

To Melinda Blau, the professionals' professional. Once again, you came through. As in any mature relationship, we bring out something different in each project, usually mirroring the topic at hand. So, in a book about adolescent-adult relationships, we took turns being soothing, empathetic, outraged, outrageous, contrite—while always pursuing the core of our project and protecting the core of our relationship.

Finally, to my wife, Stacey, whose intuitive good sense and deep compassion helped me preserve the balance I tried so hard to maintain in *The Second Family*.

Ron Taffel

In this, my third collaboration with Ron Taffel, I continue to be amazed by his genius and his generosity. Ron is truly one of the great family thinkers of our time. As a writing colleague, he is the best that one can hope for: perceptive, open to new ideas, attentive to detail, and able to discern the nuances of language and delivery. (Ron, we both know you *could* write your own book; I'm glad you have chosen instead to have me channel your wisdom and your words. The end result is an experience that defies the typical definition of co-authorship.)

I wish to thank Ron's wife, Stacey, and his children, Leah and Sam, for their support during this and all our writing projects, which sometimes cut into their family time.

To my children, Jennifer and Jeremy, and to the other "parental units," as we recently called ourselves at Jen's wedding to Peter, our newest family member, I am always grateful for your love, your interest in my work, and for your patience when deadlines loom.

Finally, and certainly not least of all, I wish to thank Eileen Cope at the Lowenstein Literary Agency, who always has the vision and intelligence to understand new ideas, and as always, a nod to Barbara Lowenstein, our seasoned and fearless leader.

Melinda Blau

About the Authors

Ron Taffel, Ph.D., is a noted child and family therapist and author of over one hundred professional and popular articles, as well as the critically acclaimed childrearing guides *Parenting by Heart, Why Parents Disagree,* and *Nurturing Good Children Now.* Dr. Taffel consults with and lectures at school, religious, and community organizations around the country. He is an award-winning contributing editor to *Parents* magazine, and the founder of Family and Couples Treatment Services at the Institute for Contemporary Psychotherapy in New York City, where he lives with his wife and children.

Melinda Blau is an award-winning journalist and author of *Watch Me Fly, Families Apart, Loving and Listening, Our Turn,* and *Secrets of the Baby Whisperer,* as well as the coauthor with Dr. Taffel of *Parenting by Heart* and *Nurturing Good Children Now.* She is the mother of two grown children and lives in Northampton, Massachusetts.